SPECIAL OPS

JOURNAL OF THE ELITE FORCES & SWAT UNITS

VOL.12

CONCORD
PUBLICATIONS COMPANY

Editor: Samuel M. Katz

by CONCORD PUBLICATIONS CO.
603-609 Castle Peak Road
Kong Nam Industrial Building
10/F, B1, Tsuen Wan
New Territories, Hong Kong
www.concord-publications.com

We welcome authors who can help expand our range of books. If you would like to submit material, please feel free to contact us.

We are always on the look-out for new, unpublished photos for this series. If you have photos or slides or information you feel may be useful to future volumes, please send them to us for possible future publication. Full photo credits will be given upon publication.

ISBN 962-361-663-5
printed in Hong Kong

Middle East Crisis 2000
The Regional and Global Dangers

When, on September 13, 1993, Israeli Prime Minister Yitzhak Rabin accepted the open hand of PLO Chairman Yasir Arafat in an epic handshake that was once considered unthinkable, the promise of peace in a land crippled by war seemed a tangible reality. For some sixty years, Arabs and Jews have been locked in an unforgiving conflict over control of a small strip of land that sits between the Jordan River and the Mediterranean. The State of Israel and her Arab neighbors have, until that momentous handshake, squared off in six full-scale wars. For thirty-five years, the Palestinians have waged an unnerving terrorist war against the Jewish State and her interests around the globe. Too many had died on both sides for the war to go on. The time had come for, in a biblical call for sanity, to beat swords into ploughshares.

There were reasons why both sides had come to the bargaining table after years of life in the trenches. The Soviet Union, long a manipulator of the situation to exacerbate regional tensions in a Cold War chess match fought with the blood of others, had evaporated into a bankrupted shambles. The United States, the sole superpower remaining, had just come off its masterfully waged war in the Persian Gulf. Not only had Saddam Hussein been defeated, but the U.S. was now in a position to convince the Arab States that the time was ripe for their constructive roles in settling the Arab-Israeli conflict. The PLO, a liberation organization that straddled the fence between Third World liberation movement and international terrorist movement, was bankrupt. Yasir Arafat had, backing the wrong horse, openly sided with the Iraqis during the Gulf War. When the conflict ended, so too did the hundreds of millions of Kuwaiti and Saudi petro-dollars that kept the PLO in business. Israel, in Prime Minister Yitzhak Rabin, was led by a former general and highly respected founding father who might have been the only politician capable of selling peace with the Palestinians to a wary public. Sensing that its longtime foe was weakened, Israel embarked on peace.

What had shown so much promise in 1993 endured seven years of prolonged haggling and bargaining. The Israeli peace effort survived the assassination of Rabin and a two years terrorist suicide-bombing campaign. The Palestinian peace effort survived the brief regime of Prime Minister Netanyahu. What the peace process could not survive was the unsettled issue Jerusalem.

In the summer of 2000, Prime Minister Ehud Barak offered the Palestinians what in Israeli-circles had been a taboo subject—part ownership of areas near Jerusalem for a future capital of a Palestinian State. Barak was considerably weakened politically by his offer of Jerusalem, as foes in the Knesset abandoned his ruling coalition. Arafat scoffed the proposal, wanting Palestinian sovereignty over the entire eastern half of the holy city. Soon talk of a holy war for the liberation of Jerusalem was heard in the Palestinian media. All that was needed was a spark.

On September 28, 2000, opposition Likud-party leader Ariel Sharon, a pronounced opponent to the peace process, marched to the Temple Mount in Jerusalem, along with 1,000 policemen and Shin Bet agents providing him with much need security. The Temple Mount stood between the Wailing Wall, the holiest site in the world for Jews and the Dome of the Rock mosque, the third holiest site in the world for Muslims and a living symbol of nationalism for the Palestinian people. The "Jerusalem Intifadah" had begun.

Along no-man's land that separated two partners in peace, Beirut-style gun battles erupted. Palestinian youths, urged on by Arafat's political party, took to the front lines. The bloodshed was horrific, as were the acts of barbarism. The conflict reached a boiling point when a mob of Palestinian lynched two Israeli soldiers in Ramallah. Israel responded by launching helicopter gunships against targets throughout the West Bank and the Gaza Strip, including strikes against Arafat's offices in Gaza.

The pace by which the crisis escalated into open warfare shocked political leaders in capitals from Jerusalem to Washington D.C. A fight over Jerusalem was used by terrorists in Beirut and Afghanistan as an open call to wage a holy war against Israel and the United States. Along Israel's northern border with Lebanon, Hizbollah brazenly kidnapped three Israeli soldiers on patrol. In the port of Aden, in Yemen, the U.S.S. *Cole* was attacked by two suicide-bombers and seventeen sailors were killed in the blast. American embassies all over the world were placed on high alert. Law enforcement officials in the United States expect that the wave of violence in the Middle East to inevitably find its way to its shores.

In this issue of Special Ops Journal, we have assembled a cross-section of unit profiles of the players in this regional conflict that has turned into a global threat. The units featured here have been important tools in the Middle East's past and present conflicts and they are also on guard in case that conflicts spread to the four corners of the globe.

Samuel M. Katz - October 2000

Heroes in Kevlar

The Washington D.C. Metropolitan Police Department Bomb Unit

Samuel M. Katz

After successfully cutting the device's power source from a well-concealed battery, the two bomb techs retreat toward the command post to be decontaminated.

To anyone who wears a badge, especially to those whose primary mission is to battle terrorists, the world is a very small place. An incident in the alleyways of Gaza or a call for a Jihad in the caves of Afghanistan can manifest themselves into bloodshed on the streets of our cities. The term "global village" is an apt description of how boundaries have been obliterated by air travel and immigration.

When, on October 12, 2000, the first sketchy reports of the suicide attack on the U.S.S. Cole were reported on CNN, a small group of law enforcement specialists in the District of Colombia sat stone faced staring at the screen. These officers, veterans of the trench warfare that is counter-terrorism, realized that this was yet another bloody probing action in yet another campaign of the prolonged terrorist war waged against the United States. Vigilance would be heightened and targets—and there are many in the small terrain they patrol—would seem so much more vulnerable. Every time leaders of the Islamic Jihad or Hamas called for a holy war, or at each cease-fire collapse along the front-lines in the West Bank, the officers realized that the fuse grows shorter.

The Washington D.C. Metropolitan Police Department Unit emblem.

The Washington D.C. Metropolitan Police Department Unit patch.

Nighttime comes with a sparkle of regal brilliance to Pennsylvania Avenue. With an opulence that the capital city of the world's last remaining superpower deserves, Washington D.C. takes on a floodlit feeling of power and urgency once darkness overtakes the city center. At the West Wing entrance to the White House, adorned in a bright picture postcard yellow glow, the scene is absolute frenetic. White House staffers, wearing ID tags around their necks, race in and out of the west gate as uniformed officers of the U.S. Secret Service man their vigilant posts. Along the cordoned off roadway that borders the outskirts of the White House, the preparations for a "move" are underway. Special Forces officers from the U.S. Parks Police in full tactical kit assemble to cordon off the federal parkland around the White House. A hovering U.S. Parks Police chopper circles overhead securing the route and searching rooftops, as a large convoy of Secret Service follow cars and support vehicles move in. The armored armada that will take President Clinton the quarter mile from the White House to the Hilton Hotel will shut down a portion of Washington D.C. in a fast-moving swarm designed to safeguard the Commander in Chief from harm. At the front of that armada, searching the route for any possible explosive devices, will be the Washington D.C. Metropolitan Police Department Bomb Unit.

Moments before the presidential "package" departs the West Wing, Officer Paul Friedlander from the Bomb Unit races ahead up Pennsylvania Avenue on the route the motorcade will take. The role of the "bomb car" is simple—search the route for any object, from a mailbox that looks tampered with to a truck that seems out of place that appears suspicious. The bomb technician must then make a quick determination to see if the suspect item is, indeed, an explosive device and then must take immediate action. A special agent from the U.S. Secret Service joins Officer Friedlander in his run to coordinate command and control communications with the presidential motorcade "just in case."

One of the unit's EOD vehicles stands at the ready outside the White House.

All along Pennsylvania Avenue, leading to Washington Circle and then to the site where the President would be speaking, officers from the Metropolitan Police Special Operations Division, from Harbor Unit officers to Emergency Response Team SWAT cops, are deployed at strategic intersections. Presidential moves are part and parcel of the natural landscape in Washington D.C. and an equally deterring force secures each move. The bomb car, however, is considered the lynchpin of the package. If a suspect item is found, then the bomb technician will have to rely on his experience, training and nerves of steel to render it safe or at least remove it from the president's path.

Evening traffic in downtown Washington D.C. is pushed aside as the presidential departure nears. Driving ahead of the presidential motorcade, the officers scan the surrounding avenues for anything that might be out of place. There is no hindsight in this all-important mission. No second chances.

The typical Washington D.C. Metropolitan Police Department Bomb Unit patrol and response vehicle.

During a bomb-scare on a busy overpass near Georgetown, responding police units await the arrival of the Washington D.C. Metropolitan Police Department Bomb Unit.

Officer Paul Friedlander, one of the most experienced EOD technicians in the unit, locates a Federal Express truck that is double-parked picking up the evening's packages. "Move this vehicle now!" Officer Friedlander instructs the driver, "and now means ten seconds ago." Anything along the route that sparks suspicion is given the once over. From Beirut to Bogota, Belfast to Sri Lanka, terrorists have used car bombs with great effectiveness. Working the bomb car is a source of great stress for the officers, even when one considers that they render safe explosive devices for a living. Protecting the President of the United States from an assassin's bomb is a daunting task. That sense of urgency and mission is increased a hundred-fold at times when rage throughout the Middle East is directed at the United States and the President in particular.

Arriving at the "site," the Washington Hilton where President Reagan was shot nearly twenty years earlier, the officers scan the nearby surroundings as the presidential limousine arrives. For the D.C. Bomb Unit this has become routine, but routine can, at any moment, be interrupted by sheer terror. "My job ends when the president returns to the White House," one of the bomb technicians working the detail explains, "until then making sure his path to wherever he goes is safe and secure is my sole mission."

It takes a special kind of police officer to put himself between the citizens he is sworn to protect and serve and a volatile and powerful explosive device. Yet in Washington D.C., where government offices and embassies make ideal terrorist targets, the elite Washington D.C. Metropolitan Police Department Bomb Unit has proven to be a Kevlar shield of protection to the United States of America's most target rich city. To a terrorist, there are few metropolitan areas as tempting as

After having had his route "swept" by the Washington D.C. Metropolitan Police Department Bomb Unit, President Clinton arrives at a speaking engagement some ten blocks from the White House.

Always prepared to meet any threat before it can harm the President, the Washington D.C. Metropolitan Police Department Bomb Unit "bomb car" is parked next to one of the Presidential limousines near the Convention Center.

Officer Paul Friedlander checks out the area next to the President's departure point for anything suspicious.

Washington D.C. Home to the President of the United States, congress, and dozens of other government and public service offices, as well as some 150 embassies and foreign missions, our nation's capital is inside the cross-hairs of any group or individual eager to kill or maim in the name of a cause. And the terrorists' favorite weapon is the bomb. Explosive devices, whether wrapped around the torso of a suicide-bomber, packed in the trunk of a car or manipulated into a mailed package, have been used to terrorize individuals and countries. They have maimed and they have murdered. And, as the World Trade Center and Oklahoma City bombings have proven, the United States is not immune from random death on the streets of its towns and cities. The indiscriminate destructive might of the terrorist's bombs has literally shattered our national and natural senses of security.

Washington D.C. is a unique city. There are nearly a dozen law enforcement agencies operating in the D.C. area, though the Metropolitan Police is the primary force protecting and serving the city's citizens and government agencies. The Bomb Unit, with its dozen or so officers, is one of the busiest in the world. Beyond the presidential runs (they do about 300 a year) they spearhead and work examining and rendering safe suspicious devices called in by citizens or law enforcement entities, they also supervise the transportation of any and all explosive material moving through Washington D.C. The workload for the small team is enormous. Sometimes it is mind-boggling especially when considering that the unit is so small.

On January 2, 1997, four letter bombs arrived at the Washington D.C. bureau office of Cairo's *Al-Hayat* newspaper. All the letter bombs bore a December 21, 1996 Alexandria, Egypt postmark and contained no return address. These bombs were in plain white envelopes, with computer-generated addresses. There were other markings on the envelopes yet inside, the envelopes packed a lethal load. The Christmas cards that were inserted into the envelopes contained tiny circuit boards designed to play music when opened, were modified to create a final circuit in the detonation of letter bombs. An explosive filler, thin and rolled, was fitted with a detonator and the wiring tied into the musical circuit board. The explosives carried in each of the envelope could easily have ripped off a limb or blown off someone's head .

"No words can describe what goes through your mind when you come up against a real terrorist bomb," reflects Officer Louis Rivera, an experienced veteran of the unit, "let alone three or four at one time. All you can think of is your training and your experience and most of all your standard operating procedures. Great care, on any bomb run, is taken to ensure officer safety. Unlike the Hollywood stereotype of a EOD work, bomb technicians do not render devices safe with a wire clipper in one hand while guessing if the red or white wire needs to be cut. There is no guesswork involved in the dangerous assignment of turning a potentially lethal bomb into an inert package and hand's-on handling is a matter of last resort. For the most part, the Washington D.C. Metropolitan Police Department Bomb Unit relies on "disrupters," or electrically charged mini-cannons, to fire a round through the mechanism of a possible bomb and disrupt or destroy its electronic circuitry. "Once you remove the power source from an initiator, you have won half the battle," claims a unit bomb tech. Bomb officers wear heavy Kevlar layers of protection before even examining a suspicious package. Once an actual device is handled and must be transported for safe disposal, the unit deploys a state-of-the-art "Total Containment Vehicle" (or TCV). The round cannonball-like device, with hydraulic lifts that can be driven to and from the bomb location, provides maximum safety at a device's most volatile moments of transport. The exact specifications of this unique piece of machinery are classified top-secret for the obvious reasons though the most important "stat" about TCV, claims one of the unit officers is "that we trust it!" After all, as unit commander Sergeant Roger Blair notes,

Officer John Turner confers with Officer Paul Friedlander (seated) prior to a "Presidential" run.

Following the successful bomb run with the Secret Service and the Washington D.C. Metropolitan Police Department Bomb Unit, the President's limousine returns to the White House.

A Washington D.C. Metropolitan Police Department Bomb Unit response car awaits the Secret Service and the President for an evening run to a speaking engagement.

"Equipment and tools can always be replaced but people can't!"

Kevlar and Plexiglas provide an outer layer of protection against "conventional" explosive devices, but today the major concern facing units like the Washington D.C. Metropolitan Police Department Bomb Unit are weapons of mass destruction. The 1995 Tokyo Sarin gas attack was a wake-up call heard loud and hard throughout American law enforcement that fanatic groups had no hesitation about deploying weapons of mass destruction to further their cause. Yet perhaps even more ominous to American law enforcement was the arrests, in Amman,

Working as a well-rehearsed team, Bomb Unit personnel assist an officer to suit up.

During a call, a Washington D.C. Metropolitan Police Department Bomb Unit officer readies the team's gear for a render safe procedure.

Jordan, of over twenty terrorists from Osama Bin-Laden's al-Qaida organization, who would later be convicted of planning to attack American and Israeli tourist targets in Jordan prior to the millennium celebrations. The attacks weren't just going to be the "run-of-the-mill" massacre or bombing. Bin-Laden's lieutenants had planned to attack their targets, intelligence officials charged, with a series of bombs armed with chemical payloads.

The desire of the Bin-Laden network to raise the ante of violence by using a non-conventional weapon was seen as a major development in how American interests around the world—as well as targets *inside* the United States—would be targeted. When Bin-Laden's terrorists would, like the bombing of the World Trade Center in February 1993, target the United States, law enforcement EOD teams wanted to be ready. And, with the White House, Capital, and a multitude of governmental offices all blocks from one another, Washington D.C. was determined to be ready.

In recent years, there have been numerous false alarms. On April 24, 1997, a mail clerk at the national headquarters of the Jewish *B'nai Brith* social organization discovered a suspicious package in the mailroom. The clerk duly placed the manila envelope in a wastepaper basket and then phoned police. When responding units arrived, they were initially apprehensive to call the Bomb Unit—the package did not bear the telltale signs of a letter bomb. There were no restrictive markings on the packet, it wasn't mailed from a foreign country and there were no strange odors or oily stains on the manila envelope. When patrol officers opened the package, they found a shattered petri dish covered in plastic bubble wrapping. The small dish was labeled with the word "Anthrax" spelled wrong, as well as the word "Yersina," a lethal bacterium that causes the bubonic plague. Also inside the package, the officers found a two-page letter warning that the manila envelope contained a "chemical weapon." By the time the contents of the dish were analyzed and deemed benign by a FBI lab, a massive response had been summoned to *B'nai Brith*

Officer Louis Rivera (standing) and Officer Paul Friedlander examine an x-ray of potential WMD package during an exercise in southern Washington.

Under the careful eye of a fellow EOD technician, the two Washington D.C. Metropolitan Police Department Bomb Unit EOD techs suit up in their protective suits.

headquarters involving fire, police and the Bomb Unit. What could have been a lethal attack that killed hundreds or more turned out to be nothing more than a hoax.

For the men and women of the Bomb Unit, however, the dreaded call of a real weapon of mass destruction call-out is a chilling reality of the job. Working in a nuclear, biological, or chemical environment is a completely different universe than anything most EOD units are trained to handle. Unlike a small pipe bomb, which could very well kill the bomb tech and hurt those in their immediate surroundings, a small packet containing a chemical or biological ingredient could kill tens of thousands. To train for that scenario, the unit runs routine drills in which a suspicious device deemed to contain either a biological or chemical agent must be rendered safe.

On the shores of the Anacostia River, on a bright and breezy winter morning, the Washington D.C. Metropolitan Police Department's Bomb Unit responds to a call of a suspicious box left near a phone booth. Upon closer inspection, the officers discover that the box contains a vile of liquid attached to a timer, wires and what looks like a detonator. The bomb techs will need to be very careful when handling this device. Tackling a weapon of mass destructive (WMD) device is nothing like

The cumbersome, almost prohibitive WMD-level protective suit must be worn underneath the heavy Kevlar bomb suit on all calls of a suspicious device that may contain chemical or biological agents.

Working carefully and methodically, a bomb tech from the Washington D.C. Metropolitan Police Department Bomb Unit helps his fellow officers slither into their Kevlar cocoons. On all calls, officers can live or die with the reliability of their protective gear. On WMD calls, that reliance is increased a thousand-fold.

The responding Washington D.C. Metropolitan Police Department Bomb Unit EOD techs carefully check on their Scott-pack breathing apparatus that will provide them with a secure source of breathable air. Like divers about to depart for the abyss of uncharted waters, the teamwork that each EOD officer exhibits is as valuable a survival tool as are his protective garments and disrupter devices.

rendering safe a "conventional" bomb. The usual tools that the Bomb Unit would employ, such as a disrupter, could not be employed as the charge fired to disrupt the device's power source could invariably release and spread the WMD agents. Rendering a WMD device inert requires a hand's on approach where the EOD tech must get up close and personal with the agent and its detonating mechanism.

Looking like a spaceman who landed smack dab in the middle of battle, a Washington D.C. Metropolitan Police Department Bomb Unit EOD tech attempts to search for a power source and an initiating detonator on a package suspected of carrying WMD agents.

Gathering their gear for the job at hand, the two WMD-ready bomb techs maneuver through a parking lot command post toward the suspect devices.

The two officers tasked with rendering the device safe realize that the standard operating procedures that apply to conventional devices will not apply for this assignment. Underneath the cumbersome eighty pounds of Kevlar that the bomb techs wear when approaching a suspect device, the officers will have to wear a Level III protective suit that protects all exposed skin areas from exposure to the active agent. The protective suits are suffocating and restrictive. And, when worn underneath the Kevlar cocoon that must also be worn, an officer's movements and stamina are severely restricted. When handling a WMD device, the bomb techs will work in a tandem. If the elements overcome one officer it is his partner's responsibility to yank him to safety. Each officer's life hinges on his ability to work in silent unison with his partner.

Careful not to jostle or disrupt the volatile WMD agent, the two bomb techs attempt to fit themselves into a comfortable working position.

Dehydrating at a faster rate than a man wearing a fur coat in the desert's sun, Officer Louis Rivera searches for the physical and mental stamina to continue with rendering safe a sophisticated WMD training bomb.

Sophisticated chemical and biological analysis tools are crucial in allowing the bomb tech to know exactly what he might be up against.

The heavy Kevlar shell that Washington D.C. Metropolitan Police Department Bomb Unit is designed to deflect much of the power of a blast away from the officer's extremities. Yet the weight and size of the suit clearly restricts free movement.

Walking slowly from the unit's equipment vehicle, the two officers traverse a thirty-yard path toward the device. Movement is slow and cumbersome. The protective suit, looking like an astronaut's space suit, shimmers underneath the olive Kevlar wrap that cover both bomb techs. On a cool day, an average size man can dehydrate inside the suit in less than fifteen minutes. In the often-unbearable humid and suffocating Washington summer, moving inside the suits, let alone using one's hands to gingerly neutralize a device that could kill scores of people, is inconceivable.

Both officers examine the device as they kneel on the ground gesturing to one another with hand signals. A power source is located and a wire leading from it to the small glass test-tube like container is located and cut. WMD exercises are designed to assess response times, strategies, and an officer's ability to work inside such a restrictive protective environment. Although physically and psychologically challenging for the bomb techs, each time the unit watches CNN in its quarters, it realizes that threats and capabilities emanating from oversize might one day emerge in their precincts.

Officer Paul Friedlander rides in on the unit's TCV during a bomb call near the police academy.

It is morning in Washington D.C., the height of the morning's rush, and President Bill Clinton is scheduled to make an appearance some ten blocks from the White House away at the Washington Convention Center. Even the quickest of "moves" requires a Herculean security effort and like they do so many times, the Washington D.C. Metropolitan Police Department Bomb Unit is in the vanguard of the security package. Officer John Turner, an experienced unit veteran is assigned the bomb car this bright and sunny morning, along with a Secret Service agent. In case a vehicle needs to be examined for explosives, a Secret Service K-9 team is on hand, as well. Although Secret Service dogs are used for presidential moves, the D.C. bomb unit is one of the few EOD units in the country to cross-train its bomb techs and K-9 handlers into one cohesive team. Because of security concerns stemming from the Middle East, the atmosphere of routine is replaced by heightened awareness.

Driving ahead of the motorcade, Officer Turner examines the route and a delivery truck with great scrutiny—better safe than sorry is a policy that keeps people alive in EOD work. As he arrives at the destination and deems the route to be clean, Officer Turner listens for the sirens of the approaching motorcade. The armada of black limousines, decoy carts, follow cars and support and emergency vehicles demonstrates the very real threats that the President faces even in Washington D.C. It also demonstrates that need for vigilance and a squad of highly-trained EOD professionals ready to serve on the front lines of the new war that is American counter-terrorism.

"Fred," one of the unit's bomb-sniffing dogs observes as his master and partner suit up for a bomb call.

ISRAEL'S UNDERCOVER COUNTER-TERRORIST UNITS

Samuel M. Katz

Lining up in an assault stack, undercover operators race around a building for what is known in the unit as "the deciding explosive moment."

Friday, October 13, 2000—Ramallah, the Palestinian Authority. The images on television sets throughout Israel were abhorrent. Two Israeli reservists, having taken a wrong turn near a jagged no-man's land separating Israel from the Palestinian Authority, were shepherded by Palestinian police to the city's police station for "safe-keeping." Crowds of protesters, however, returning from a funeral of a boy killed by Israeli gunfire, heard of the two "soldiers" in police custody and demanded vengeance. A call for mob retribution soon turned into an uncontrollable frenzy of violence that, even by Middle Eastern standards, was shocking. The two Israeli soldiers were lynched and savagely beaten to death in an orgy of ripped flesh and spilled blood. When one of the dead soldiers was tossed out of the second story window of the police station, faces inside the room where he had been beaten to death emerged to show their proud faces and display their hands soaked in their prey's blood.

Israeli attack choppers would respond in kind and turn the Ramallah Police Station into a pile of smoldering rubble. But TOW-missile tit-for-tat would hardly bring about justice or send a message to future mob leaders.

In Israel, at military and police bases throughout the country where special operations units honed their skills, commanders reviewed the tape of the lynching over and over again in absolute disbelief. They could only wonder how, in a day and age of high-resolution television and imagery where a face in the crowd with blood on his hands could easily be identified by the intelligence services, could a cold-blooded killer be so brazen as to advertise his crime to a global audience. Israel has, on numerous occasion's, used its covert commandos to exact justice on those terrorists whose crimes were so brutal and so unforgiving that required the special talents of men who move about in darkness, in disguise and armed to terminate any threat. From Tunis to Beirut, Israel had expressed its determination that killers would not sleep soundly in their beds.

On a chilly autumn night near the frontier with Ramallah, a force of men in disguise disappeared into the darkness armed with sidearms, assault rifles and up-to-the-minute intelligence on those they hunted. A few days later, reports in the Israeli press surfaced that many of those responsible for the lynching in Ramallah, including the young man who displayed his blood-soaked hands to the world, had "somehow" been returned to Israel to face justice.

Although made famous, or infamous as some claim, as a result of their infiltration and counter-terrorist operations during the Palestinian's first Intifadah (1987-1993), Israelis have been disguising themselves as Arabs for nearly a hundred years in the unstoppable cycle of violence of the Arab-Israeli conflict. A *Mista'arev* is someone who isn't an Arab by origin, but due to various reasons dresses in Arab garb, acts in accordance with Arab manners and customs, speaks Arabic, and lives where most of the population is Arab. The term *Mista'arvim* is derived from the Arabic expression of *Musta'arvim*, or "intervening." The first Israeli *Mista'arvim* date back to 1909 and the "*Shomer*," an organization designed to provide security to the first Jewish settlements in Palestine. *Shomer* guards rode Arabian horses, dressed in traditional Arab garments, and learned to speak fluent Arabic to not only gain the respect of their neighbors, and to find out what they were up to. The *Haganah*, the military arm of the Jewish settlements in pre-independence Israel, created its own Arabist intelligence unit during the bloody Arab revolt of 1936-39, when agents in Arab garb were dispatched to infiltrate local Arab

Armed with "his" Jericho pistol, an undercover commando dressed as a woman takes aim on a Hamas hideout.

During infiltration exercises "near" the West Bank, an undercover operative plays the part of a Hamas activist. With the intelligence services of the Palestinian Authority moving about Gaza and the West Bank in plain clothes, often armed with M16s and AK-47s, the undercover teams have found carrying their weapons while on assignments in Palestinian areas to be a bit easier.

villages. During the Second World War, a *Haganah* Arabist platoon called "the Syrian Company" was set up with British support to carry out sabotage missions deep behind Vichy lines in Syria and Lebanon. Most of the volunteers to this small, though unique unit were of Oriental descent—men whose families had come from the Arab Diaspora and who were fluent in Arabic and Arab customs. Commanded by Captain N. N. Hammond, an eccentric British intelligence officer and professor of Greek history at Cambridge, the Syrian Company received extensive small arms, sharp-shooting, demolition, communications, and hand-to-hand combat training, as well as intensive Arab language, customs and culture instructions. Another "Arabist" unit was *Shachar* ("Dawn"), more a force of intelligence plants than commandos, who penetrated large work sites to gather information and recruit double-agents; they also opened small cover businesses and peddler stands at Arab markets to camouflage their activities. Many of these agents transferred to the Shin Bet and the Mossad, to carry out intelligence and special operations.

Yet Israel's first taste of undercover warfare in the counter-terrorist arena came during the bloody campaign to neutralize the Gaza Strip in 1970, when the Israel Defense Forces (IDF) formed a small, though very active, unit simply as "Pomegranate Recon." Created by the rambunctious and controversial OC Southern Command at the time, Major-General Ariel "Arik" Sharon, Pomegranate would prove to be as revolutionary as they were decisively effective. Three years following the 1967 Six-Day War victory and capture of the Gaza Strip from Egypt, Israel ruled the densely populated squalor in name only. Heavily armed terrorists openly carried their weapons through the streets and alleyways of the strip and its refugee camps, and bloody attacks against Israeli soldiers and civilians were daily occurrences. The IDF, an army that only a few years back humbled the entire Arab world, could not conquer a few hundred hard core terrorists. Pomegranate Recon was formed to change the equation. A small force of only a few dozen men, Pomegranate Recon was commanded by a visionary special operations officer named Captain Meir Dagan who realized that conventional means could never defeat an unconventional army entrenched inside a million hostile souls. Together with a concentrated effort by agents from the Shin Bet, Captain Dagan and his men *became* what they hunted. "When you are in Gaza act like you are from Gaza" was a unit catchword. Unit operators not only dressed as local Arabs, but also disguised themselves as terrorists, moving through populated areas clutching Soviet-made assault rifles and Carl Gustav submachine guns. The undercover operators infiltrated the terrorists' world by eating in their restaurants, shopping in their markets, even staking out their whorehouses. They made the terrorists uneasy and unsure to move freely in territory they claimed as their own. The terrorists never knew who to trust, where to walk, and when they might be ambushed. In tactical operations, the commandos from "Pomegranate Recon" performed with speed, precision and overpowering firepower. Advance teams would infiltrate a location, secure entry and evacuation routes, and create an "opening" for the assault element. Terrorists who were "lucky" were captured without a shot being fired and rushed to an interrogation facility. Those who resisted were often cut down in a flurry of gunfire.

In one remarkable year, "Pomegranate Recon" crushed the terrorist uprising in Gaza. They killed hundreds of terrorists, destroyed intelligence networks, and blew up safe houses and arms caches. Pomegranate Recon brought a subdued peace to Gaza that lasted until the eruption of the Intifadah in December 1987 when, once again, an

Two undercover operators man a front line observation outpost near a village with a strong Hamas presence.

undercover campaign to combat terrorism was needed by an army unwilling to use oppressive force and an enemy unwilling to be humbled by anything less.

Even before the first Palestinian uprising began, Major-General Ehud Barak, then OC Central Command, felt that the IDF needed a special operations element inside the territories. In early 1987, months before the outbreak of the Intifadah, Barak authorized the establishment of an undercover unit, to be known as "*Duvdevan*," or "Cherry," that would operate in the West Bank as a covert intelligence and strike force. The first soldiers in the unit, all volunteers, were graduates of the Paratroop Brigade's squad commanders' course, and were later given a complete undercover instruction regimen including a "disguise course," counter-terrorist training, and intensive instruction in Arabic and Palestinian customs. A second undercover unit, responsible for the Gaza Strip, was also formed. Because of the difficulty in apprehending known and wanted terrorists in an area as dense and ripe for violence as the Gaza Strip, the struggle was considered one of biblical proportions. And, as a result, that undercover unit would be known as *"Shimshon,"* or "Samson," after the biblical hero who fought the Philistines in Gaza.

From 1988 to 1994, the IDF's two undercover squads were the busiest units in the entire IDF. They deployed daily, and nightly, for ambushes, intelligence-gathering forays and arrests. The list of fugitive and known terrorists wanted in 1990, for example, included hundreds of names in the West Bank alone—by 1993, only a few dozen names remained on "West Bank's Most Wanted." Many terrorists preferred to surrender to security forces, or escape to Jordan and Egypt rather than find themselves behind the crosshairs of an undercover soldier's weapon. Nearly 200 Palestinians terrorists were killed in undercover unit ambushes, including some of the most dangerous—and fanatic—Hamas operatives the IDF has ever faced in battle. Wanted terrorists never felt safe on the streets of Gaza, Ramallah or Hebron. They never knew which face in the crowd was covered by theatrical make-up? Was the old woman with the groceries actually a twenty-year-old sergeant with an Uzi, or a mother of nine living in a refugee camp? Was the old-man with a can and pronounced limp a respected town elder, or was he a young Tel Aviv native about to produce a gun and a set of handcuffs.

Operators from an undercover "back-up" team suit up with tactical assault vests, ladders, and emergency medical gear.

Taking aim with his Micro-Uzi submachine gun at one of the unit's training facilities in central Israel, a "blonde-haired" IDF undercover officer prepares to empty a thirty-round magazine-emptying burst.

Although most Palestinians considered the undercover units to be nothing more than masquerading murderers, those involved in the struggle, including those now in the security hierarchy of Arafat's Palestinian Authority, grudgingly admit that the undercover units were instrumental in breaking the back of the Intifadah. "These soldiers used ruthless and provocative measures to infiltrate our villages and towns," a senior commander of the Palestinian intelligence services commented to a visiting American security official, "but their methods were ultimately successful."

The units were so successful, in fact, and the work so overwhelming that additional undercover units were also created. The National Police Border Guards, also tasked with security operations inside the territories (as well as inside Israel proper), created its own undercover squad, known by the acronym of "*Ya'mas*," or *"Yehidat Mista'arvim."* The Jerusalem Police, needing to fight an increased terrorist presence inside the Old City (particularly around Temple Mount) as well as the villages in Arab East Jerusalem, also created its own undercover unit called "*Gideon*."

Poised in position for an assault on terrorist, a squad of undercover operatives await the order to 'attack!"

Conscripts eager for slots in the IDF's undercover unit undergo extensive psychological profiles. According to some published reports, the selection process weeds out 99 out of every 100 volunteers. Any soldier who has had a family member hurt or killed in a terrorist attack is automatically disqualified from volunteering into the unit. Most of the volunteers into the army's units come from the country's Kibbutz and Moshav collective farms. For these soldiers, many of whom are blonde and blue-eyed, service in an undercover squad presents a double challenge. Not only do they need to prove their worth as combat operatives in training in order to make it in the unit, they also need to try twice as hard to adopt the cultural and physical masquerade needed to successfully infiltrate Palestinian areas. Most of the volunteers into the Border Guards' *Ya'mas* have an easier go of it—they come from households where Arabic is a second language and the Oriental traditions were second nature. The Border Guards, because of its large number of Ethiopians in its ranks, have been able to recruit policemen who, as seen in the operation in Nablus, could openly pose as Sudanese and other North African migrants. Published accounts have also recently revealed that the *Ya'mas* has utilized the services and courage of a remarkable and very striking blonde policewoman. In one operation, the undercover policewoman produced a high-powered weapon from a revealing outfit, and captured one of the most wanted Hamas terrorists on the West Bank.

An undercover operator displays his M4 5.56mm assault rifle fitted with a reflex sight.

The qualities sought after in an undercover unit candidate are more mental than physical, explains one Israeli special operations officer. "Any number of young kids have the physical where-with-all to parachute out of an airplane, run for twenty kilometers at a stretch, or march up a mountain with fifty kilograms on his back. But only a small minority of men have the mental stamina to learn how to assume a foreign identity, cultivate it into a believable act, and then combine these acting and intelligence skills, with that of a proficient special operations commando." According to one operator, "Being an undercover operative is a state of mind more than being a good shot or able to toss a grenade

"Y," the unit commander and whose identity is protected for security reasons, briefs his squad of operators prior to a live-fire-training scenario.

through a bunker's opening. Sure I am trained to leap out of a vehicle and, in a split second, have my weapon trained on a wanted terrorist, but if I can't pass myself as one of them, I am not worth the costume I am issued with. I have to know how to talk like them, look like them, eat like them, laugh like them and even smell like them. I must know that if an old woman passes me in street I must respectfully move to the left, and if an old man passes me, I should greet him with the words '*Salaam, Aleikum*' ("Peace Be Onto You"). I must think in Arabic, react in Arabic, and ensure that the masquerade remains strong until the green light is given, my weapon is produced, and my true identity is finally compromised to the locals. If I get out of character for even one small second before the mission begins, I not only endanger myself and my team, but the back-up

An undercover operator, part of a rear cover force, takes aim with his M4 5.56mm assault rifle during a training exercise.

Weapons safety, either in a training scenario, or in the middle of an Arab village on an operation, is maintained with religious dedication in the undercover squads.

force and a lot of innocent Palestinians who could wind up in the middle of a fire fight. My acting abilities won't earn me an Academy award, but it will save lives and reduce the need for firepower to its absolute minimum."

Training for an undercover soldier is lengthy, and is dedicated to intelligence work, the art of masquerading, the "Arabization" of the fighter (from learning traditional customs and culture to intensive language instruction). The undercover candidates are immersed in everything and anything Palestinian—from the slang used by common laborers to the words to popular songs—from a commercial frequently aired on Palestinian radio to a popular song honoring slain Hamas master bomb-maker Yehiyah Ayyash, known to the world as "The Engineer." Arabic cannot be second nature, it must be a primary persona. They must think in Arabic, react in Arabic, and functions as Arabs; many trainees return home on leave only to find themselves talking to parents and friends in Arabic. Only after the operator has mastered his new identity can intensive close-quarter combat instructions commence. Soldiers are taught advanced assault skills, as well as some of the more refined aspects of plain-clothes work. Speed is always stressed over firepower and guile and surprise is always preferred over brute force and prolonged. All undercover unit operators are expert marksman, proficient in the martial arts, and recipients of advanced medical and communications training. All undercover operators are equipped with sophisticated communications equipment in various sizes which enable the soldiers to maintain communication links among themselves and with backup units, even at long ranges.

The ideal undercover unit operation is one in which no shots are fired, but Murphy's Law is as much a part of special operations as is the pumping surges of adrenaline, the kick of fear, and the cold metal of a CAR-15 assault rifle. To prevent casualties, exhaustive preparation is mounted prior to each operation. Undercover operators rehearse their

Gaining the element of surprise in a Palestinian van driven by operators disguised as a married couple, heavily armed operators leap from a screeching vehicle.

roles in particular operations over and over until they have it just right. Precision must be split second, and firepower directed solely at those who are armed. Speed is essential, the soldiers must be able to remove their garments, produce their weapons and assume control of any situation in a blink of the eye; during a fire-fight, they must know how to change their weapon's magazine in an instantaneous, almost second-nature, reflexive move. Speed on the trigger finger must not mean indiscriminate firing. Before every operation, from an assault on a targeted home to a simple reconnaissance assignment, the undercover team always meet the regular soldiers of the rescue force face to face. The rescue force, heavily armed and wearing body armor, is briefed, and told when to and not open fire. Bitter experience has shown that being mistaken as a Palestinian can have tragic consequences. Many undercover operators have been too good at their trade for their own good. Friendly fire incidents have occurred and operators have been killed.

Recently, the bloody reality of how an undercover operation can go bad came on August 27, 2000 when three operators from "*Duvdevan*" were killed by friendly sniper fire during a daring midnight raid in the village of Atzira Shamali, near the West Bank City of Nablus. The undercover squad had operated in the village for weeks in the hope of capturing Mahmoud Abu Hanoud, a twenty-eight-year-old Hamas commander wanted for a series of bombings in Jerusalem. When the undercover squad stormed Abu Hanoud's safe house and gunfire erupted, the operators pursued the Hamas cell leader to the building's rooftop. The soldiers were not supposed to follow Abu Hanoud to the roof, a series of snipers that ringed the house were to take him out should he attempt to flee. But in the heat of battle when volleys of automatic weapons fire often interrupt communications, the snipers opened up on the men wearing *kefiyah* headdresses on the roof. Abu Hanoud was wounded by a sniper's bullet and managed to escape to the Palestinian Authority. The sniper fire cut down the three Duvdevan commandos, as well.

The botched raid in Atzira Shamali was a turning point. Hamas viewed the Israeli fiasco as a weakening of the covert anvil that had struck their underground with such unforgiving effectiveness. Inside Israel, too, the friendly fire deaths were the source of great infighting and introspection. "How can we expect eighteen-year-old kids to execute

Undercover unit snipers, adorned in their camouflage smocks, discuss a pre-mission deployment.

During rioting in Hebron, a young paratrooper takes aim with his M4 5.56mm assault rifle. (Yves Debay)

In Hebron, where the undercover teams have been incredibly busy, an IDF paratrooper displays a Palestinian flag seized from rioting youth. (Yves Debay)

missions of such grave national importance, all alone, inside Palestinian territory," a mother of a soldier in the unit lamented on an Israeli radio call-in show. Some retired commando officers, veterans of raids on Entebbe and Beirut, were even quoted as saying that the undercover operations were simply too dangerous. There were even calls to disband the undercover teams altogether—though those calls died on September 27, 2000, when the "Super Intifadah" was born.

When all hell broke loose along the front lines of territory separating Israel from her autonomous Palestinian neighbors, the undercover squads were among the first thrown into the fire. Teams were secreted into Palestinian areas to locate sniper positions and report on the complicity of Arafat's political and police forces in instigating the violence. The Palestinians feared the exploits of the undercover teams to the point that Palestinian intelligence agents would mingle with the crowds on the front lines, eager to capture the disguised Israelis in the act. In fact, fear of the undercover operatives was so great that when Palestinian police in Ramallah detained two Israeli reservists who had wandered into town by accident, the rumor in the city on edge was that an undercover tandem had been seized. Word spread throughout the town already boiling to frenzy with rage. Hours later, a mob of Palestinians stormed the police station and lynched the two Israeli soldiers.

It is just after dawn at the *Ya'mas* training base in Central Israel, and under the watchful eye of a short and lanky man carrying a Mini-Uzi and a stopwatch, a small squad of undercover operatives perform a dry run on

An ancient street ideal for guerrilla warfare and counter-terrorist operations—the narrow alleyways of Hebron. (Yves Debay)

In Hebron, an IDF officer confers with local residents in an attempt to lessen the violence. (Yves Debay)

During training for a reconnaissance sortie in territory jointly patrolled by Israeli and Palestinian forces, two Ya'mas operators carrying concealed cameras act as consumers as they scout an area behind a fruit stand.

Operators, some in tactical kit and others in disguise, discuss a tactical scenario inside the unit "kill house."

A Ya'mas commander (center) briefs a squad of operator prior to a mission.

the combat assault course. In less than twenty-four-hours they will once again cross the murky frontier separating the State of Israel from the Palestinian Authority. The objective of their preparation and eventual disappearance into the anonymity of a Hamas-controlled village is a terrorist commander who intelligence has learned is planning a string of suicide bombings to further exacerbate tensions between Prime Minister Ehud Barak and Palestinian Chairman Yasir Arafat. The Shin Bet, Israel's secret service, believes that the target is roaming the countryside between Israeli and Palestinian-controlled territory utilizing a library of forged identify cards, a bag of disguises, and enough cash and support to keep him invisible from both the Israeli and Palestinian security forces. A resident of a West Bank town near Israeli lines, the terrorist is considered wily, resourceful, heavily armed and extremely dangerous. Each man in the *Ya'mas* team realized that the target is unlikely to surrender and would rather martyr himself than be snared in an Israeli undercover operation; he was known to be both brutal and strict. During quiet times the mission is considered high-risk. In the atmosphere of the open warfare now transpiring, some seasoned veterans view the operation as "borderline insanity".

After the early morning rehearsal and some fine tuning of tactics that the unit commander wants perfected, the men attend to the task of readying their disguises, cleaning their weapons, and pondering the long night ahead in enemy territory. They realize the dangers they'll be facing soon, and ponder the horror of lying mortally wounded on a dust-strewn alleyway in the PA area. "Ask any one of these men what they rather be doing—working undercover in the West Bank or enjoying peace and the universal response will be peace," claims a senior Border Guard officer. "Yet as long as there is no peace, with both sides shooting at one another and the suicide bombers vowing to blow up women and children, these men will don their disguises, hide their weapons, and live and die by their wits and courage so that others can be safe!"

An undercover operator in full tactical kit hoists a ladder before a dry run of an assault.

Prior to a rehearsal for an actual operation later that evening, an undercover tactical squad suits up in their load bearing vests.

Attack! Ya'mas operators perfect the intricate split-second art of assaulting a fortified terrorist location.

With his Jericho automatic at the ready, an operator on a ladder slowly pulls himself up toward a firing position.

Climbing inside a house, this operator readies his Jericho automatic.

Close-up photograph of an operator and his helmet illumination system—ideal for the chaos of close quarter battle on a dark West Bank night.

Lined up outside a targeted location in "text book manner" with weapons at the ready, an undercover squad awaits the order to attack.

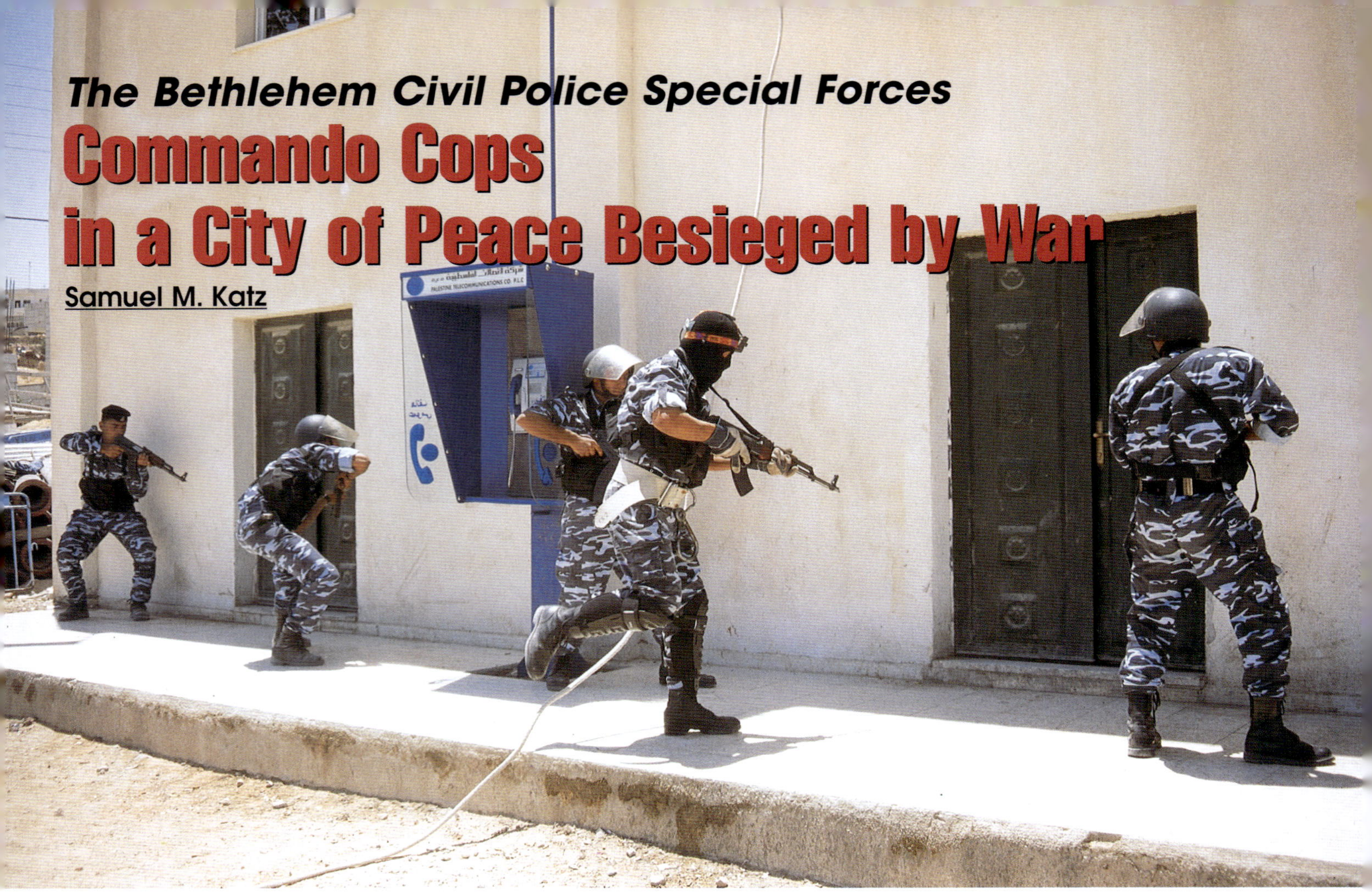

The Bethlehem Civil Police Special Forces

Commando Cops in a City of Peace Besieged by War

Samuel M. Katz

Poised for an entry and ready to crush any resistance, an assault element prepares to storm a terrorist location.

Dateline Bethlehem, the Palestinian Authority. The smell of gunpowder was unmistakable, as was the choking stench of burning tires and blood in the streets. In October 2000, at a time when the final details of a final and long-lasting peace between the Israelis and the Palestinians was supposed to have been in the final stages of high-level negotiation, full-scale war had erupted.

At a junction along a dusty street, the bustle of a morning's rush hour moved slowly through the arteries of the city. Traffic heading toward Joseph Rachel's Tomb was bottlenecked at the Israeli checkpoint. Cars and trucks heading toward Manger Square were snarled in gridlock caused by twentieth century vehicular traffic crowding streets designed for mules and camels. Traffic cops, in white sailor-like uniforms, attempted to move the cars and trucks along where a traffic light had ceased functioning, though a squad of nearly thirty cops were poised for action in a half dozen Land Rovers and vans. The officers armed with AK-47 assault rifles and wearing blue and white urban camouflage fatigues were focused on an orange Fiat slinking its way toward the light. This was an ambush—West Bank style—and the tactical cops maintained close radio communications with the commanding officer, whose voice grew dryer with anticipation as the targeted vehicle moved closer toward the preplanned ambush position. When the commander shouted "Go!" the officers suddenly leapt from their vehicles with weapons at the ready and ran toward the Fiat. Within seconds, a dozen men armed with assault

Atop the police station in Bethlehem, a Special Forces cop mans his post.

The all-terrain Land Rover, ideal for the hills and winding steep roads of Bethlehem, is the primary transport tool of the Bethlehem Civil Police Special Forces.

During hostage-rescue training, a Bethlehem Civil Police Special Forces operator negotiates a rooftop ladder.

rifles ringed the surrounded compact, as an officer opened the driver's side door and yanked the driver out onto the pavement. Following a rudimentary search, the driver was handcuffed and tossed into the back of a Land Rover and the ride to police headquarters. The takedown, a drill for the massive security operations that would precede Pope John Paul II's pilgrimage to Bethlehem, took all of two minutes.

Two thousand years ago, wise men and shepherds gathered in

Following a briefing in the operations center of the Bethlehem Police Station, Civil Police Special Forces march toward their vehicles.

Wearing the standard urban-pattern camouflage fatigues and what the Palestinian police special forces wear as a tactical load bearing vest, a Bethlehem Civil Police Special Forces cop is briefed prior to an operational assignment.

Bethlehem to worship a child that promised peace on earth and goodwill for all. The Bethlehem of today is a very different place. Bethlehem lies a handful of kilometers south of Israeli capital Jerusalem, 765 meters above sea level in a dry and inhospitable terrain. The city, carved out along an ancient caravan route, was always a mosaic of many cultures that traveled to and from Jerusalem and the other cities in the ancient land. Today, the city is at ground zero along explosive lines of separation near the embattled epicenter of the Arab-Israeli conflict.

Suited up and ready for battle, Civil Police Special Forces prepare to deploy in their Land Rovers to a trouble spot near the Deheishe Refugee Camp.

During a training exercise, Bethlehem Civil Police Special Forces race into action.

With weapons raised ready to terminate any threat, Special Forces cops surround a targeted terrorist location.

Bethlehem is a city of contrasts. It is the birthplace of Christianity though the city is predominantly Muslim. The City of Bethlehem is one of the most important religious and tourist cities in the West Bank, a city that boasts peace and goodwill, yet it sits on a holy war fault line that now pits potential partners for peace in the first volleys of full-scale war. Bethlehem is a city of 24,000 inhabitants, surrounded by a string of refugee camps and villages that push the district's total population to nearly 150,000. Because the city's primary industry is tourism, the municipality has always taken great care and investment into organizing and maintaining the city to construct installations for the convenience of tourists and pilgrims. Because it was a historic message of peace, Bethlehem was the crown jewel of the towns under Palestinian Authority control on the West Bank. Keeping that jewel untarnished was the job of the Palestinian Civil Police and its elite special forces.

Civil and security control of Bethlehem was transferred to the Palestinians in 1995, as part of the Israel-PLO Declaration of Principles on Interim Self-Government Arrangements signed in Washington on September 13, 1993. The Declaration of Principles provided for a transitional period of Palestinian interim self-government in the Gaza Strip and the West Bank. Under the Declaration of Principles, Israel agreed to transfer certain powers and responsibilities to the Palestinian Authority, which includes a Palestinian Legislative Council and a mandate of internal security and public order in territories that the Palestinian controlled.

Internal security and public order in the areas controlled by the Palestinian Authority would fall under the auspices of a myriad of police and intelligence agencies directly under the Palestinian General Security Service, or GSS. The GSS, or "Palestinian Directorate of Police Forces," as it is officially known, was established in May 1994 with the signing by Israel and the Palestinian Authority of the Cairo Agreement. The police and subsequent intelligence services of the GSS were divided into two territorial zones of responsibility for the Gaza Strip and the West Bank. There are numerous different services that fall under the GSS umbrella. They include:

* The National Security Force (*Quwat al-Amn al-Watani*) which, with more than 14,000 officers, is the largest Palestinian security agency. Their primary mission is service along border areas separating Palestinian and Israeli control as well as inside the major cities. The National Security Force was also responsible providing officers to serve on joint-patrols with Israeli police and military forces** as well as manning checkpoints.
* The General Intelligence Service (*Mukhabbarat al-Amma*) is led by Major-General Amin al-Hindi, and is the official Palestinian Authority intelligence agency and was one of the original branches of the GSS, as delineated in the Cairo Agreement. With a current strength of about 3,000 officers, the *Mukhabbarat* is involved in intelligence gathering inside and outside the territories, counterespionage operations, and developing relations with other foreign intelligence agencies.
* Preventive Security Force (*al-Amn al-Wiqa'i*) is a plainclothes security force that operates in the West Bank and Gaza with over 5,000 agents. Considered to be the largest of the Palestinian intelligence forces, the Preventive Security Force is tasked with preventive actions against terrorist and opposition groups—primarily Hamas, the Islamic Jihad, and some of the more radical Palestinian guerrilla groups. Since its introduction and inclusion into the Palestinian order of battle, Preventive Security has been the target of numerous Human Rights groups who have accused the service of violence, abduction of civilians, interrogations, torture, and the murders of detainees.
* Military Intelligence (*Istkhabbarat al-Askariyya*) is another intelligence agency serving the Palestinian Authority, headed by Musa Arafat, that is smaller than the "General Intelligence Service." The *Istkhabbarat* is primarily a preventive service that deals with arrests and interrogations of opposition activists who might endanger the stability of the regime. The *Istkhabbarat* is one of the many controversial elements of the Palestinian police apparatus as the service is "not" mentioned in either the Cairo or Oslo II (the September 1995 Interim Agreement on the West Bank and the Gaza Strip) agreements.
* Military Police. The uniformed entity of the *Istkhabbarat*, the Military Police specializes in riot control, arrests, protection of important people and important installations, prison maintenance, and enforcement of order and discipline among the security bodies. Like the *Istkhabbarat,* this unit is not officially recognized in the Oslo Accords and is a matter of concern with the Israelis.
* The Coast Guard (*Shurta Bahariyya*) is, in Palestinian eyes, an elite unit deployed mainly in Gaza that consists of some 1,000 officers. Its official mission is to safeguard the waters off of the Gaza Strip against arms and narcotics smuggling from Egypt. Before the recent outbreak of violence, they deployed five motorboats equipped with light machine guns (the Israeli Navy destroyed these boats during their retaliatory strike against targets in Gaza). The Coast Guard's activity in the West Bank (where there is no coast) has been the source of some concern by the Palestinian Authority and international human rights groups, as officers have been involved in several notorious cases of extortion and murder.
* Civil Defense (*al-Difa'a al-Madani*) is, under its official definition, a fire department and rescue services.

The role of "conventional" policing inside the Palestinian Authority is the responsibility of the GSS's Civil Police (*al-Shurta Madaniyya*). One of the original branches of the GSS mentioned in the Cairo Agreement, the Civil Police handles ordinary police functions such as directing traffic, arresting common criminals, and keeping public order with more than 10,000 police officers in the autonomous towns of the West Bank and the Gaza Strip. According to the September 1995 Interim Agreement on the West Bank and the Gaza Strip, the Civil Police also

** Joint patrols have been suspended as a result of the Fall 2000 conflict.

Civil Police Special Forces man a roadblock along a major route through the center of Bethlehem.

deploy in twenty-five selected villages throughout the West Bank commonly known as "Area B" (areas defined as under Israeli military, but Palestinian civil control). Each city's Civil Police contingent is spearheaded by heavily armed special weapons and tactics entities known as "the Special Forces." Civil Police Special Forces units operate in each of the jurisdictions under Palestinian control and the Bethlehem unit is considered the Palestinian Authority's elite.

Prior to the outbreak of fighting in the territories on September 28, 2000, the so-called "al-Aqsa or Jerusalem Intifadah," policing in Bethlehem was considered one of the most sensitive of all public order missions inside the Palestinian Authority. Tourists, especially Christian

The Bethlehem Police Special Force's deputy commander supervises his officers moving into action.

Pilgrims, might not visit Gaza or Jericho, and they were unlikely to venture to Hebron, Jenin, Qilqiliya, Tulkarem, Nablus or even Ramallah, but a visit to Manger Square and the Church of the Nativity was a must. As a result of Bethlehem's important role as a tourist magnet, the public perception that any visitor would bring back to his native land from the newly administered Palestinian Authority would certainly stem from a visit to this holy city. As a result of the city's importance to the Palestinian Authority and the struggling local economy, the Civil Police have created a strong visible, yet unarmed presence in the city. Police officers who patrolled Manger Square did so without sidearms. Tourist Police officers, all fluent in English and some fluent in French, German and Spanish, walked a "community policing" beat inside the city center racing to offer a helping hand to any visitor in need. The Civil Police enforced public health codes to restaurants that tourists frequented and maintained a strict traffic safety program designed to limit traffic accidents, especially for overseas visitors not used to the honk-move-honk system of Middle Eastern driving. A heavy police presence inside the narrow alleyways that sport hundreds of souvenir shops was designed to dissuade pickpockets and common thieves. Family feuds, which in the area were traditionally handled with vendettas and violence, were now settled inside the police station, over a cup of sweet tea, and a warning from the police shift commander.

Yet underneath Bethlehem's veil of peace and tranquility was a city with the potential of explosive violence. The city's Deheishe Refugee Camp, with its 10,000 inhabitants living in squalor, are a source of great security concerns as it is a breeding ground for groups like Hamas and the Islamic Jihad; other refugee camps, with their pro-Hamas following, dot the district. Even inside Bethlehem Hamas graffiti and posters adorn the buildings leading to the entrance to the Church of the Nativity. Because of Bethlehem's proximity to Jerusalem and the Israeli lines, weapons smuggling is rampant in the town.

The AK-47 is the Bethlehem Civil Police Special Force's primary assault and entry weapon.

As children remain oblivious to a Civil Police Special Forces deployment in Bethlehem amid an ancient landscape, the cops deploy with weapons at the ready to block a roadway.

When Bethlehem Police Commander Colonel Abu Zaid Hadib, a long-time Arafat lieutenant, oversaw the creation of his police Special Forces squad, he realized that Bethlehem was unlike any precinct in the Palestinian Authority and that his unit would have to be ready to tackle

During hostage-rescue training in Bethlehem, a Special Forces operator glides into assault position courtesy of makeshift fast-roping gear.

Using a building's corner as cover, Bethlehem Civil Police Special Forces operators deploy during live-fire exercises.

The patch and coat of arms of the Civil Police Special Forces.

any emergency. An incident in Bethlehem, whether it was a takedown of a wanted Hamas terrorist to a gunman holding hostages would become international news. There could be no miscues in the unit's response or errors in its tactical operations. Failure could have far-reaching political implications.

Initially, when the cadre of officers that would serve as the founding members of the Palestinian Police were trained in Jordan and Egypt, little emphasis was placed on law enforcement special operations. Fledgling police departments are more concerned with laws and guidelines, uniforms and recruits, than elite 100-man SWAT units. Under the initial Israeli-Palestinian agreements, the size of the Palestinian police forces would be controlled, as would the number of guns and assault rifles each agency would be allowed to carry. Yet high-ranking officers in the police realized that the future Palestinian State would rise or fall by its ability to defeat terrorist forces determined to torpedo the peace process. Specially trained police personnel equipped with the best equipment money could buy was not a luxury but a basic necessity for survival.

In the police academies near Amman and Cairo, the very best recruits earmarked for the Special Forces were sent for advanced police tactical training. Rappelling and hostage-rescue replaced traffic tickets and building ordinances on the curriculum. Great emphasis was placed on weapons proficiency, evasive driving techniques, and close-quarter combat. Great emphasis was also placed on the martial arts and non-lethal tactics and equipment—the Special Forces, among other tasks, would be responsible for riot dispersal.

Near the unit's home facility in the center of town on a broiling summer's day, the Special Forces are hard at work executing a twelve-hour training regimen. Half the unit, suited up in riot gear, creates a human wall of camouflage fatigues and Plexiglas shields to confront a dozen police officers playing the role of rioters. The rioters hurl tin drums and rocks at the Special Forces cops, though the police lines do not crack. In fact, in tactics combined from training the unit had received in Jordan,

A Civil Police Special Forces cop prepares to provide cover fire during a hostage-rescue exercise.

After a "terrorist" suspect has been captured, he is rushed to police headquarters for a serious chat with Palestinian intelligence officials and police interrogators.

along with expertise taught from an international army of instructors, the Special Forces slowly march forward, meticulously regaining every inch of territory from the angry mob. Wooden truncheons, usually the most effective tool in dispersing a Middle Eastern mob worth its salt, remain sheathed, until the rioters can be boxed into a trap where all avenues of escape are cut off by responding police units. Because of the potential for any small riot or protest to turn into a major street-battle covered live on CNN, local police commanders give anti-riot training great importance.

At another corner of the sprawling police facility, another element of the unit is engaged in dynamic entry training. The scenario is simple—the police surround the home of a wanted Hamas terrorist only to have the suspect takes hostages in the process. The solution is not simple—Hamas terrorists are not known for their fondness of hostage-negotiators. The key to ending any tactical assignment against terrorists on the West Bank is speed and firepower. The speed to surround a targeted location will achieve surprise and security. The speed needed to gain access to rooftops and doorways is also essential in ending an incident without the terrorists getting the upper hand. Finally, if lethal force is needed, overwhelming and dedicated firepower is the great equalizer.

The assault on the terrorist safehouse commences with a small armada of fast moving Land Rovers that race to the location at top speed. Before the brakes are applied, a half dozen officers leap out of each vehicle to surround the building. Several officers from the rappelling cadre remove a makeshift wooden ladder out of their vehicle and, covered by their fellow officers, climb to the rooftop of the two-story building. AK-47s are locked and loaded and gin sights trained on all windows and doors. As the operation commander, a captain talking softly into his radio, coordinating the deployment of his men, the order to attack is issued. Officers kick in the main doors on the ground floor as several officers rappel into a second-floor window. The entire assault requires absolute coordination and weapons discipline. It also lasts all of 100 seconds. On the ground, the commander is satisfied with the training scenario, though wants to see it done faster.

Compared to Western police tactical teams, and compared to their counterparts in Israel, the Bethlehem Civil Police Special Forces are poorly equipped. Few of the officers are equipped with state-of-the-art anything—from protective load bearing equipment to rudimentary tactical assault gear such as ladders, diversionary devices, or protective shields, the tools are purely primitive. But for the missions at hand, and the difficult terrain they patrol, the Bethlehem Police Special Forces make up for their shortcomings by absolute dedication and exuberance.

Following the successful completion of an operational assignment, a Civil Police Special Forces operator raises two AK-47s in victory. Note ChiCom ammunition pouches modified for the unit's use.

And exuberance has yielded dividends. The Bethlehem Civil Police Special Forces have performed remarkably well in providing a highly visible security blanket to many large-scale gatherings in the city. Every year, the Palestinian Civil Police overseas security for three large-scale Christmas celebrations attended by tens of thousands of pilgrims. The Western observance, televised live to a global audience, occurs on December 25 (according to the Gregorian calendar); the Greek and Russian Orthodox is celebrated on January 6 (according to the older Julian calendar); and, the Armenian observance is on January 19. Crowds of up to 100,000 visitors and tourists from around the world cram the square from the morning to watch the procession of marching boy scouts and choirs. Midnight Mass is conducted in the presence of dignitaries and diplomats from all over the region.

Prior to these celebrations, the Civil Police, led by the Special Forces, conduct security sweeps of the areas. The officers are positioned in and around the entrances to the Church of the Nativity, while plain clothes agents from the police, as well as the other security departments of the GSS are also deployed to ensure that any attempted trouble is quickly neutralized. In case of any terrorist attack, a cadre of officers already suited up in tactical gear, is ready to respond to any incident.

The Civil Police's true test came on March 22, 2000, when Pope John Paul II visited the city. The Pope's visit just after the New Year was the largest security undertaking ever in the region—for both the Israelis and the Palestinians. For the Israelis, safeguarding the pontiff was of the absolute national importance while the Palestinians viewed the Pope's security on their turf as a rite of passage. Indeed, cooperation between the

Elements of the Civil Police Special Forces pose in front of the Church of the Nativity.

Israeli Shin Bet and their counterparts in the Palestinian Authority was strong—remarkable, in fact, when one considers the events of September and October 2000. On the ground, however, in Manger Square, it was the Civil Police Special Forces that were in the vanguard. The 100 men of the unit spearheaded the massive security umbrella mounted by the various police and intelligence branches of the Palestinian security apparatus. Inside the Bethlehem district, the Special Forces were the tactical spear used by the intelligence agencies in storming suspected terrorist safehouses and residences, as well as manning roadblocks tasked with bringing fugitive suspects to justice. As Bethlehem's residents were busy decorating streets with palm branches, flowers, and Palestinian and Vatican flags, the Special Forces were kicking down doors and making sure that any terrorists foolish enough to remain in the city for the Pope's arrival were in police custody. Incredible security plans were in place for the Pope's visit to the Deheisheh refugee camp, as well. "The most important thing for us was that the Pope came and left without any incident," a Special Forces officer reflected, "our mission was to prevent any act that could have been a spark in the path toward conflict."

At sunset, on a warm summer's day, a contingent of Civil Police Special Forces officers march in formation in front of the Church of the Nativity. In front of the holy site, the officers parade unarmed, but the message of their presence in Manger Square is unmistakable. In the city where Jesus was born, these men are the rule of law. That adherence to the rule of law will have to apply to the Civil Police and all the security elements long after the Palestinians march on this, an apparent last bloody spasm, before statehood.

During a "deterrent patrol," Civil Police Special Forces personnel march in Manger Square.

Hamas and Hizbollah posters plastered at the entrance of the Church of the Nativity.

Police Special Forces teams deploy for action near the Deheishe Refugee Camp.

A Bethlehem Civil Police Special Forces captain takes aim with his AK-47 during an operational assignment on the outskirts of the city.

After receiving word of a possible hostage-incident near the entrance to Manger Square, officers from the Bethlehem Civil Police Special Forces race from their living quarters to their response vehicles.

A Special Forces police officer salutes a lieutenant during a mission near the Deheishe Refugee Camp.

Footnote

For the first few weeks of the fighting in what the Palestinians called the "Jerusalem," or "al-Aqsa Intifadah," Bethlehem remained one of the quieter locations on the front lines. Anti-Israeli rock-throwing incidents were low compared to border checkpoints in and around Gaza and on the West Bank in Ramallah, but armed elements of Fatah militiamen and policemen in plain clothes did fire upon Israeli neighborhoods in Gilo, in Jerusalem. Even after Palestinian Civil Police Special Forces in Ramallah failed to protect two Israeli army reservists who strayed into the city from a mob that eventually lynched them, police in Bethlehem attempted to keep tensions and incidents to a subdued level of rage.

On October 19, 2000, however, a large and powerful explosion rocked police headquarters in Bethlehem killing two officers. Initial reactions among Palestinians led residents to believe that Israeli forces had shelled the city or had used helicopters against targets there. It soon became evident, however, that the massive explosion occurred when, according to Israeli sources, two men working on behalf of Arafat's protective service were in the process of preparing a bomb, which exploded and set fire to the propane gas canisters. Another scenario considered likely is that the blast may have occurred during an attempt to dismantle a bomb confiscated from a Palestinian guerrilla organization.

On October 23, 2000, Bethlehem became the front lines of the violence. Israeli military forces blockaded the town of Beit Jalla in the Bethlehem district after Palestinian gunmen have been firing into a Jewish neighborhood of Jerusalem. Palestinian sniper positions in Beit Jalla were pummeled by IDF machine-gun fire from tanks and infantry, and TOW missiles were launched from helicopter gunships. A factory in Beit Jalla was destroyed and Bethlehem was plunged into darkness after power lines were severed.

In November, the fighting in Beit Jalla and around the city's frontiers with Israel intensified.

Special Forces personnel patrol the entrance to the Church of the Nativity.

During a dignitary protection detail in Manger Square, a Special Forces officer supports his comrades in the regular "blue" police.

America's First Line of Defense

The U.S. Marine Corps Security Guard Battalions

Samuel M. Katz

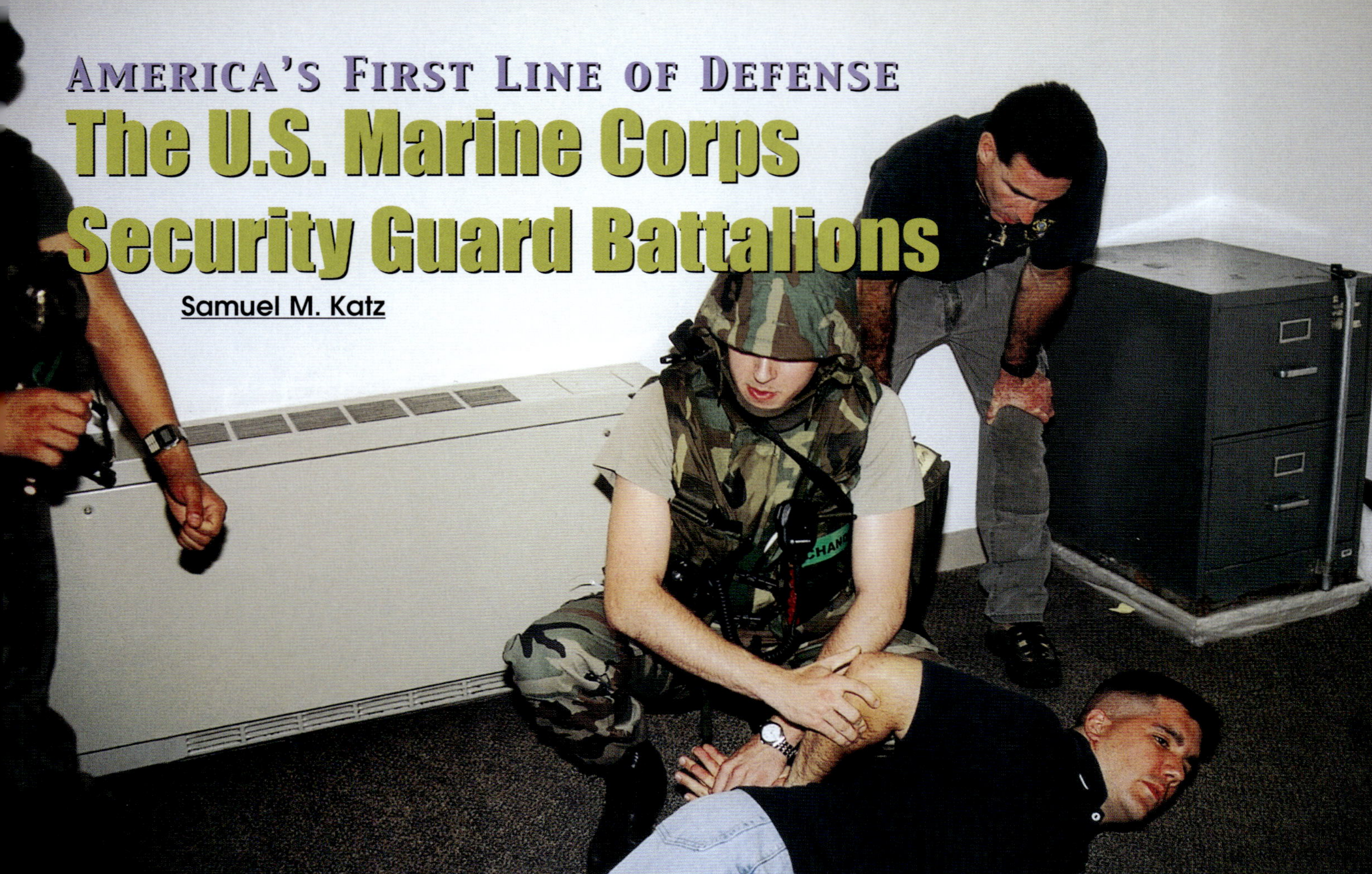

A DSS MSD instructor looks on as a MSG's "cuffing" techniques are reviewed.

"Every Clime, Every Place!" – The MSG Motto

Dateline Cairo, October 13, 2000. Outside the Embassy of the United States, in front of the North Gate at 8, Kamal e-Din Salah Street, the crowds of protesters had swelled far beyond to what Egyptian police had prepared for. Imams in the city's grand mosques had just delivered a morning's full of fiery sermons denouncing Israel for its use of force against the Palestinians, and against the United States of America, for supporting the Jewish State. Egyptian riot police, in their black fatigues and Plexiglas shields, were braced for trouble and for a fight—bamboo batons were used with bloody results against protesters who attempted to push toward the front gate of the sprawling American embassy. Inside the diplomatic post, America's largest embassy overseas, tensions were high. The stench of dissipating tear gas and burning American flags had overtaken much of the compound. Inside the fortified embassy buildings, the men and women of the Marine Security Guard contingent manned their posts in tactical gear prepared for any contingencies. Less than twenty-four hours earlier, seventeen of their comrades in arms had been killed on board the U.S.S. Cole *when two suicide bombers rammed the vessel in the port of Aden, Yemen. Only a few days earlier, a mob of government-incited rioters had stormed the U.S. embassy in Damascus, Syria, in a violent expression of rage against American support of Israel. Tensions in the region were high and, from Beirut to Islamabad, Nairobi to Dar es-Salaam, terrorists had already killed hundreds by attacking American embassies all over the world. After all, an embassy is a symbol of all the United States stands for.*

The mission of the Marine Security Guards, or MSGs, is to provide "internal" security to State Department missions (an embassy, consulate or legation) around the world, to prevent the compromise of classified material, and to provide protection for United States citizens and United States Government property. These missions are commonly referred to as a "post" and overall security for these installations is the mandate of the U.S. State Department's Diplomatic Security Service and the Regional Security Officers (RSO). In only the most extreme emergency situations are they authorized duties exterior to the buildings or to provide special protection to the senior diplomatic officer off of the diplomatic compound. The MSGs are in the front lines of some of the most volatile regions on the four corners of the globe ready, at a moment's notice, to face overwhelming numbers in the defense of their posts. The Marine Security Guards are also tasked to provide special guard services for U.S. delegation offices for regional or international conferences at which classified information is kept and assist in guarding the temporary overseas residences of the President, Vice President, or Secretary of State.

At a diplomatic post, the detachment commander and RSO form the Post Security Team. Their relationship is the key to the security program's success. The RSO is overall responsible for all internal and external security programs, as well as all background and criminal investigations. The detachment commander is ultimately responsible to the Chief of Mission, but normally reports to the RSO on day-to-day issues. At larger posts with several RSOs, the detachment may report to one of the Assistant RSOs.

The United States Marine Corps' working relationship with the State Department began some 200 years ago when, in 1799, a detachment of Marines protected Consul General Edward Stevens while he conducted negotiations with Haitian rebel leader Toussaint L'Ouverture and French officials. In 1805, in a campaign that has been immortalized in the Marine Corps hymn, a landing party of Marines waged a ferocious battle in Tripoli to restore the flag to the battered American consulate, as well as free the captive crew of the U.S.S. *Philadelphia*. During the Marine's mission to Tripoli, they restored the Pasha to the throne of the kingdom who, in turn, rewarded one of the Marine officers with a jeweled sword.

A Marine Security Guard stands guard outside of "Post One" at the U.S. embassy in Madrid, Spain.

During their role in suppressing piracy in the Caribbean and South America in the 1830s, Marines guarded the American mission in Lima, Peru. In 1842, Marines organized the first consular guard in Shanghai.

Throughout the last 150 years, Marines have responded to threats against American posts and missions throughout the world, serving in Argentina, India, Honduras, Japan, Korea, Egypt, Lebanon, Abyssinia, and the Philippines. The Marines' most famous intervention to safeguard an American mission came in 1900, in China, during the Boxer rebellion. As a response to an anti-foreigner wave of rage that spread throughout China, a Marine contingent fought its way to Peking to, against overwhelming odds, hold off repeated hordes of attackers for fifty-five days until relief arrived.

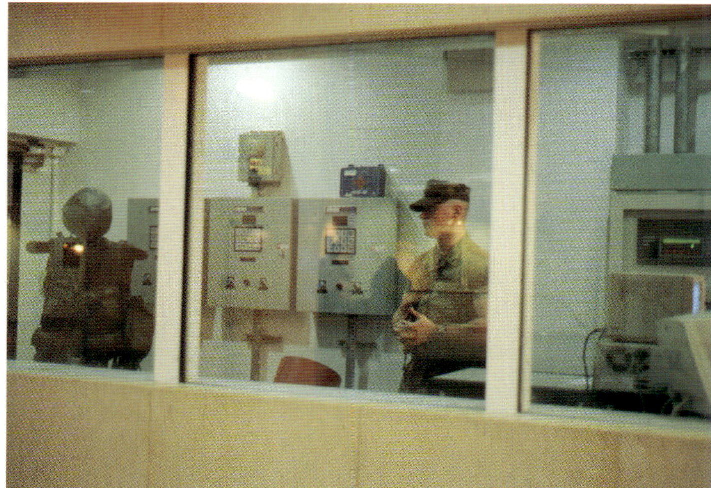

"Post Two," U.S. Embassy, Cairo, Egypt. Each "post" is a fortified mini-bunker and communications center from where defense of a besieged embassy can be led and coordinated.

With a baton at the ready, a MSG radios in his position during a roving patrol in front of "Post One" in the U.S. Embassy in Madrid, Spain.

The Marine Security Guards program of today dates back to the Second World War when a sixty-man force of Marines was rushed to the American embassy in London to provide internal security for diplomatic and military personnel. The Foreign Service Act of 1946 authorized U.S. Navy and Marine Corps personnel to serve at foreign diplomatic posts around the world. On January 28, 1949, the first MSGs departed for their posts at Tangier and Bangkok. Today, the Marine Security Guard Battalion currently fields over 1,000 Marines at 121 detachments organized into seven regional MSG companies and located in over 100 countries.

One of the U.S. State Department Diplomatic Security Service Assistant Regional Security Officers assigned to the U.S. Embassy in Cairo poses during a routine check of the MSG posts in the facility.

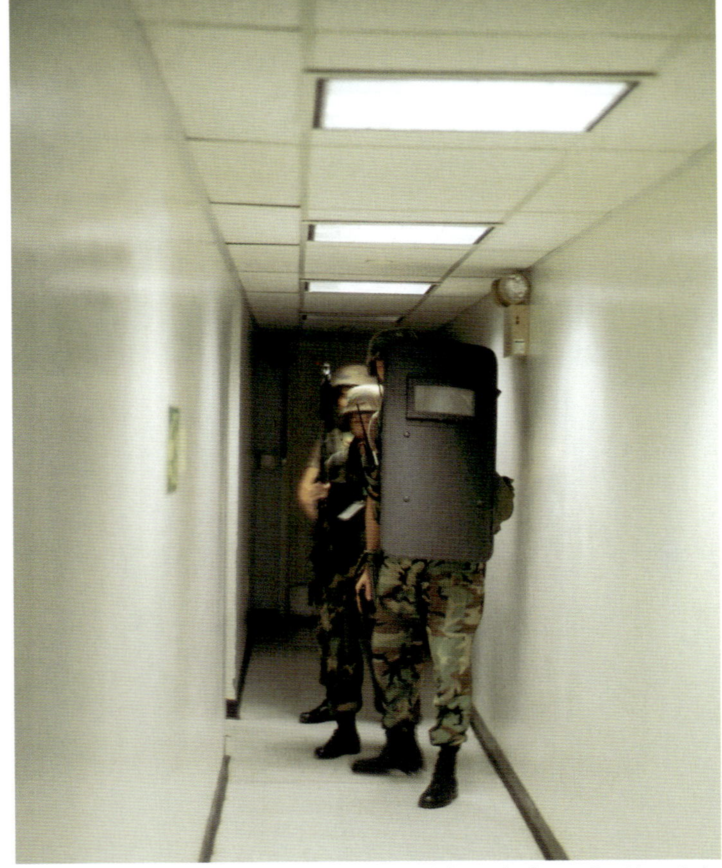

With Body Bunker in hand, MSGs retake a hallway that leads to the REACT Room during the first terrifying moments of a drill.

Headquarters Company and Battalion Headquarters is located at Marine Corps Base Quantico, Virginia. The MSG School is part of Headquarters Company. "Company A" Headquarters is located in Frankfurt, Germany and is responsible for twenty detachments in Eastern Europe, including the newly formed states of the former Soviet Union, and those emerging from the fractured chaos of the Balkans. "Company B" Headquarters is located in Nicosia, Cyprus and is responsible for eighteen detachments in North Africa and the Middle East. "Company C" Headquarters is located in Bangkok, Thailand and is responsible for eighteen detachments in the Far East, Asia and Australia. "Company D" Headquarters is located in Ft. Lauderdale, Florida, and is responsible for twenty-six detachments in Central and South America and the Caribbean. "Company E" Headquarters is located, along with "Company A," in Frankfurt, Germany, and is responsible for contingents in Western Europe, as well as in Ottawa, Canada. "Company F" Headquarters is located in Nairobi, Kenya and is responsible for eleven detachments in Sub-Saharan Africa (including the two embassies attacked in Nairobi and Dar es-Salaam). "Company G" Headquarters is located in Abidjan, Ivory Coast, and is responsible for twelve detachments in Western Africa, including those embattled posts in Sierre Leone and Liberia.

Utilizing room-clearing tactics employed by many police tactical teams throughout the United States—and throughout the world—MSGs peel off around a corner before reaching the REACT Room and securing a path for the remaining Marines in the detachment. Although the movement utilized by the MSGs when retaking a room or a floor is deliberate, speed and weapons discipline is a must.

Embassies, some mini-cities with underground passageways and all sorts of places to hide, are security nightmares—especially when a squad of MSGs must retake elements of the facility one floor at a time during a REACT drill.

As the MSGs move beyond a doorway toward the REACT room, a sergeant radios in the updated developments as well as his coordinates to the Gunnery Sergeant coordinating the REACT exercise. As one of the MSG's functions is to safeguard classified material, sensitive locations inside an embassy always receive special attention during a REACT drill.

The move and cover system of retaking a room and a floor is perfected in countless REACT drills by MSG detachments all over the world—from high-threat posts like Cairo to more glamorous American diplomatic facilities in Western Europe and Asia.

The Marine Security Guard Battalion is an elite within the Marine Corps. The mission of the MSGs is primarily defensive. MSG role is essentially defensive in nature. They serve as an in-house deterrent to limited acts of violence, as well as a defense mechanism to large-scale riots. The Marines are expected to delay entry by hostile elements long enough to permit destruction of classified material and to assist in protecting lives of the mission staff until host government forces arrive. They are authorized, under the command of the senior Foreign Service officer present, to use weapons to protect their own lives or mission staff from direct and immediate danger. Being a MSG requires nerves of steel and an adherence and dedication to mission that few soldiers possess.

Volunteers wishing to serve in the Marine Security Guard Battalion undergo a grueling highly specialized six-week training course. The MSG-hopefuls are taught intensive close-quarter combat skills, marksmanship, weapons retention and counter-terrorism. MSGs destined to be sent to counter-intelligence threat posts, such as China, various Middle Eastern countries and states in Eastern Europe, receive additional

A tandem of MSGs slowly and deliberately negotiate their way up a yet 'secured" stairwell during a REACT drill in Madrid, Spain. This Marine Security Guard raises his Beretta sidearm before clearing a doorway.

training. During the hand's on phase of the instruction, the class operates in a mock-up embassy divided into "Post One," "Post Two" and "Post Three." Post One is the name of the embassy's primary interior security post. It is normally in the lobby or main entrance of the building housing the Chief of Mission. Post One is the principal command station for all access control to the building. It is equipped with closed circuit televisions, radios, and intrusion detection and fire alarm controls. Residing behind bulletproof glass, the MSGs survey the personnel traffic and monitor the various security displays around the clock. At the larger diplomatic posts, additional security positions are in place. These fortified checkpoints may be manned twenty-four-hours-a-day or in some slower diplomatic mission, just during normal business hours. They could have a full compliment of security displays and equipment similar to Post One or could be a roving security watch after the embassy has closed.

After graduating from the School, the MSG can expect to be

MSGs always operate in small squads or even tandems when, during a REACT drill, they secure a stairwell or a room. Both the point and rear MSGs must secure the advance of the entry teams as they meticulously and often exhaustively retake an embassy.

assigned to two fifteen-month tours. Some MSGs volunteer to serve on twelve-month hardship tours to such enticing travel spots as the embassies in Beirut, Algiers and Kosovo.

Once in a post, the MSGs conduct reaction drills, called "REACTS," to their embassy for emergencies such as fires, bomb threats, bombs, intruders, riots and demonstrations. Upon reaching the embassy, they assemble in the "REACT Room" to receive orders and direction from the detachment commander. This room provides not only a storage area for weapons, ammunition, and personal protective equipment, but also a safe and secure position to suit-up for the REACT situation. Each potential REACT scenario is practiced and has its own standardized drill from which the MSGs can modify to fit the actual situation.

It is a warm night in Cairo amid an air of tension and threat that those who serve in Egypt have come to accept as part and parcel of their day-to-day existences. Egypt is a dangerous country rife with civil unrest. The country is also home to one of the most radical Islamic terrorist groups in the Middle East—one whose primary objective has been attacks against the regime of President Hosni Mubarak and the United States. That group is The Islamic Group and their spiritual leader Sheikh Omar Abdel Rahman, is currently in an American federal prison following his conviction for planning terrorist conspiracies in the New York area. The Islamic Group was responsible for the October 6, 1981, assassination of Egyptian President Anwar es-Sadat as well as an attempt on the life of President Mubarak during a visit to Ethiopia on June 26, 1995. The group also carried out an April 18, 1996 attack that killed eighteen Greek tourists, who were mistaken for Israelis, as well as an attack that killed nine German tourists and their Egyptian bus driver outside the National Antiquities Museum in Cairo on September 18, 1997. The Islamic Group also claimed responsibility for the most lethal terrorist attack ever in Egypt, the November 17, 1997 attack on tourists in the Valley of the Kings, near Luxor, that killed fifty-eight tourists and wounded twenty-six others. Few doubt their resolve to attack the U.S. embassy in Cairo—especially in the wake of the bombing of the U.S.S. *Cole*.

The U.S. embassy in Cairo, beside being America's largest overseas post, is also a mini-fortress, built after the 1983 bombing of the American embassy in Beirut to limit the effects of a suicide truck bomber. Inside the embassy, as the off-duty Marines enjoy a movie on Armed Forces television inside the Marine House (the residence inside an embassy compound where the Marine's eat and sleep), or check on their e-mail, a deafening alarm sounds throughout the facility. A team of intruders is reported inside the embassy. It's a REACT drill! A patrol force is assembled to include an entry team equipped with 12-gauge shotguns and ballistic bunkers. Their mission is to secure a path from the Marine House to the REACT Room. Moving along the corridors of the sprawling building, the Marines move in a steady and slow advance toward their armory. Securing the REACT Room is their sole mission—securing the

When an embassy is attacked or bombed, and the possibility exists that a building can lose power and be plunged into darkness, flashlight attachments to the MSG arsenal of 12-gauge shotguns can mean all the difference in the world. Compact, lethal and ideally suited for the close quarter combat environment of an embassy building, the Remington 870 is a standing favorite with MSG detachments around the world.

embassy will come later with the entire detachment. But time is a definite factor. If the intruders are a probing force of terrorists out to prepare the embassy for a larger assault, the Marine detachment must suit up and get into position.

Once the REACT Room has been secured, the detachment suits up and assembles with dire, yet well-choreographed, urgency. The detachment commander assembles his suited up force, briefs them with whatever intelligence he has, and then sends the contingent out to clear and secure the embassy of the unauthorized marauders. Armed with sidearms and Remington 870 12-gauge shotguns, ideal weapons for room clearing, the Marines clear the embassy compound floor by floor, room by room. Their search is meticulous and command and control is maintained with all the posts to coordinate the operation in an effective and cohesive manner. The detachment commanders, supervising the search effort, coordinate the movement of each search party so that the embassy grounds can be deemed "secure" in as quick a time frame as humanly possible.

Each Marine wears Kevlar body armor and load bearing equipment, along with pairs of plastic flexi-cuff restrainers. Intruders are often arrested and handed over to the host government once questioned by the Marines and other embassy security personnel. Lethal force, even in the life-and-death stakes of embassy defense, is always a measure of last resort.

Some thirty minutes after the REACT drill commenced, the intruder is located inside a third floor office. Raising his Remington 870 to the prone position, a MSG shouts, "RAISE YOUR HANDS WHERE I CAN SEE THEM. INTERLOCK YOUR FINGERS ON TOP OF YOUR HEAD AND KNEEL DOWN ON BOTH KNEES. NOW, SLOWLY, LIE

Utilizing "Secret Service" like Motorola communication attachments to his field radio, MSGs radio in their position during a REACT drill in Madrid.

This close-up photograph of a MSG's REACT kit shows to advantage the tactical equipment worn by the MSGs during heightened security operations in and around the embassy.

ON YOUR STOMACH AND DO NO RESIST!" As the west quadrant search team covers the Marine approaching the invader with weapons at the ready, a pair of flexi-cuffs is applied tightly.

The "intruder" this warm and muggy Cairo night was a special agent from the Mobile Security Division from the U.S. State Department's Diplomatic Security Service. MSD, as the Mobile Security Division is known, often tours posts around the world teaching tactical skills to MSGs and to train with them during REACT drills.

MSG's cross-training with the Mobile Security Division is important, because the two elite forces often interact in international hot spots when an embassy in a besieged country must be evacuated. The recent evacuations of the U.S. embassies in Freetown, Sierra Leone (May 1997) and Brazzaville, Congo (June 1997) were greatly facilitated by the actions of the detachments. The MSGs, along with their counterparts in MSD, organized convoys to the airport, assisted the RSOs and ARSOs to destroy classified equipment, and provided a tactical ring of armor to the embassy and its personnel in those precarious moments before evacuation.

The MSGs also must train with the elite United States Marine Corps' "FAST," or "Fleet Anti-Terrorist Security Teams," that are dispatched to

In the REACT room, the name of each Marine is labeled on his or her kit to make suiting up in case of an emergency situation a much quicker process.

"STOP! LET ME SEE YOUR HANDS!" At the conclusion of a REACT drill in Cairo, when an intruding Special Agent from the U.S. State Department's Diplomatic Security Service Mobile Security Division is eventually cornered, the lead MSG apprehends the suspect. Along with the Beretta, MSGs also use .38 and .357 revolvers for close-quarter situations.

With a pair of plastic flexi-cuffs dangling off his body armor, this MSG carries his Remington 870 12-gauge shotgun on his back during a drill in the chancery building.

terrorist attacks on embassies and other military installations around the world. Securing an embassy during the day-to-day routine of business as usual is one thing—providing that same level of security to an embassy that has been twisted into a pile of smoldering metal and brick following a suicide bombing is something different entirely.

At 10:40 A.M. on the morning of August 8, 1998, the MSGs on daily duty at the American Embassy in Nairobi, Kenya were making their rounds and standing at their posts. Outside the embassy, terrorists attempting to gain access to the underground-parking garage with a water truck filled with explosives had tossed several hand grenades at the Kenyan security barrier. When embassy personnel rushed to their windows to see the source of the explosions, the truck filled with explosives crashed into the rear wall of the embassy adjacent to the underground garage, and exploded. When the bomb exploded, the force of the blast was so devastating that it blew out almost every closed window and frame on the building. Concrete walls on all floors of the embassy buckled. The dead and the dying were trapped under the horrifically twisted rubble. According to reports, much of the structure collapsed onto the chancery's emergency generator, spilling thousands of gallons of diesel fuel into the basement of the embassy. The diesel fuel ignited and smoke and fire were billowing throughout the embassy. As injured and confused people were running out of the chancery screaming and choking, the MSG detachment raced into the smoldering chaos to look for survivors. Other Marines, in a carbon copy of the drills they had performed countless times before, suited up in their tactical kit and swept the building. After all, the MSGs did not know if the bombing was but an opening salvo of a larger assault on the embassy. Perimeters were established and MSGs, shotguns in hand, provided an impenetrable ring of security to the battered embassy for the next twenty-seven hours until the first FAST teams arrived. One MSG, Sergeant Jesse Nathan Aliganga, was killed in the bombing of the embassy.

State Department diplomats praised the heroism and tenacity of the MSGs following the bombings of the embassy in Nairobi and of the embassy in Dar es-Salaam, Tanzania. "The Marines are to be commended for how exceptionally well they performed their duties under extreme conditions of chaos and terror, a diplomat proudly claimed, "their bravery and heroism was displayed in such a confident and purposeful manner that their very presence transferred to others, allowing them to get through the situation."

Many in the State Department refer to the MSGs as "their" Ambassadors in Blue. Indeed, the image of the Marine, standing proud at his post in his BDUs, is an impressive symbol of American resolve to anyone visiting an embassy overseas. Service in the Marine Security Guard Battalion is one of the most unique experiences in the American military. MSGs travel around the world and see and experience sites and history that most of their counterparts in the Corps could only but imagine. But that adventure can, sometimes, be interrupted by explosive moments of terror.

It is early morning in the office-like U.S. embassy in Madrid, Spain, and employees and diplomats slowly walk in to begin yet another day of work as America's overseas representatives. As the diplomats and other personnel enter the fortified facility, already having passed through the stringent security procedures outside the embassy and at the main gate, the MSG at Post One screens each person's pass as he controls access in and out of the building. From the port of Aden in Yemen to embassies in the Persian Gulf and Southeast Asia, the heightened security threat has raised everyone's level of readiness and concern. MSGs operate in a high-threat environment every day and over the years, from the overrun U.S. embassy in Islamabad to the attacked embassy in Saigon, twelve MSGs have been killed in the line of duty. For the MSG at Post One in Madrid, as well as his counterparts in Post Ones throughout the world, it is business as usual. History has taught the MSGs that vigilance is a key to survival as well as part and parcel of their sacrosanct mission.

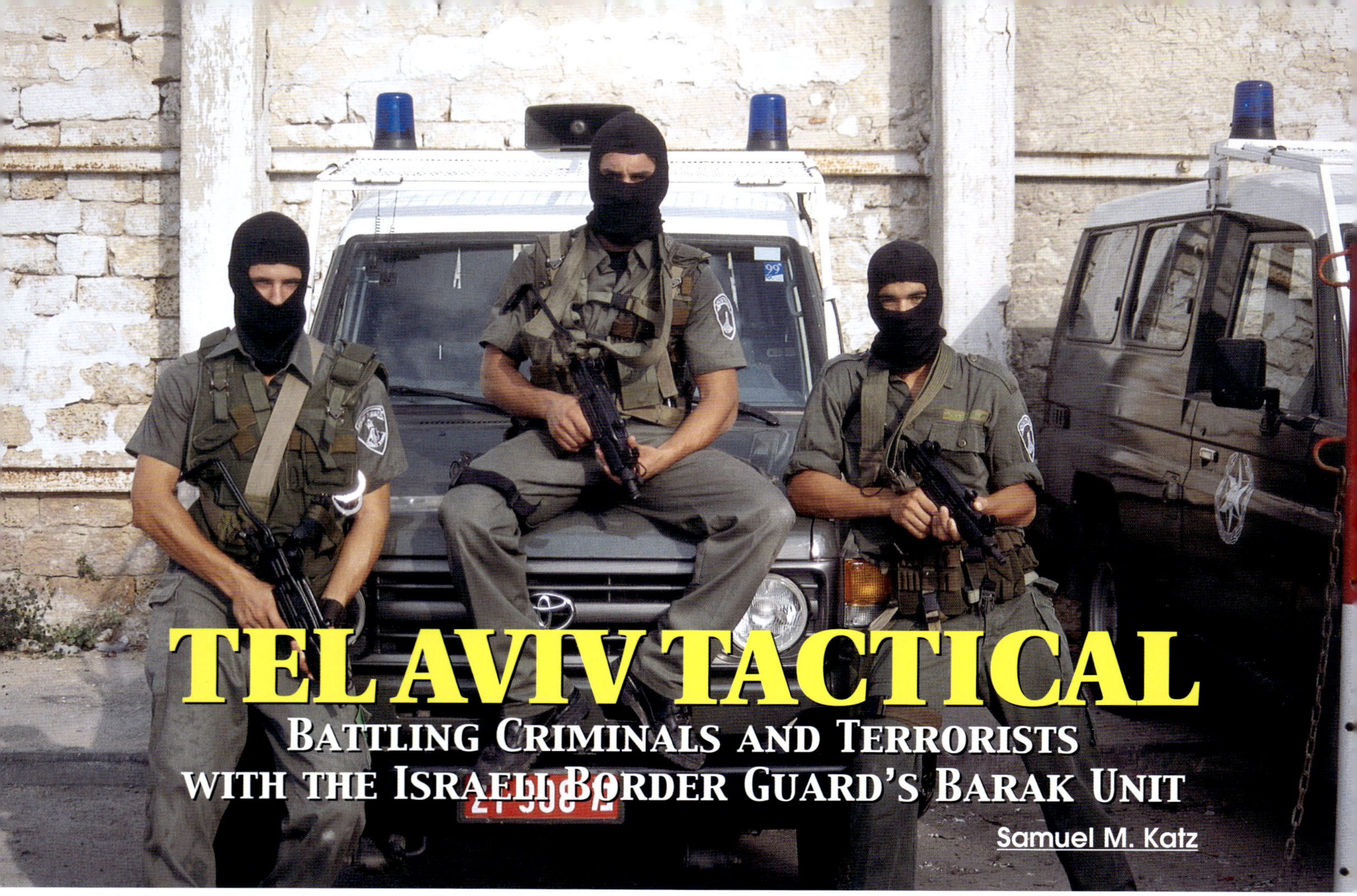

TEL AVIV TACTICAL

Battling Criminals and Terrorists with the Israeli Border Guard's Barak Unit

Samuel M. Katz

Prior to executing a series of drug raids throughout the Jaffa/Holon/Bat Yam salient, a group of Barak officers pose on the hood of their marked Toyota Land Cruiser.

Under the merciless Israeli sun in a valley in the hills of Samaria, a Border Guard instructor, sage green fatigues caked by sand and sweat, stands with his stopwatch in hand. The sounds of gunfire have resonated throughout the ancient valley near Beit Horon since dawn, though some seven hours later there is still work to be done before breaking for lunch. As the instructor wipes an endless stream of sweat from underneath his bright green beret, and juggles the summons of a pager and the endless ringing of a cellular phone worn as kit on his utility belt, his class of Border Guard officers commence an assault on a live-fire obstacle course. The combat obstacle course consists of a series of cutout targets crisscrossed along a fifty-meter long path. Each target with a balloon is a "bad guy" and worthy of at least one round of 9mm fire from the officers' Jericho 941s. The exercise is designed to familiarize the officer with what it will be like in those frantic and chaotic seconds of a firefight when movement, cool nerves and accuracy will result in innocent lives being saved and guilty souls being blown away. The sun glares cruelly into the eyes of each officer as he, and she, embarks on the quick drill, making it hard to stare down on a target for more than a fraction of a second. The Jericho 941 holds sixteen rounds and there are sixteen targets with balloons on the course. Each round is meant to count and the policemen, especially in this unit, are not supposed to miss.

The Israeli National Police patch.

The Israeli Border Guard patch.

For the next week, the officers will embark on a series of exercises that will include storming barricaded buses and buildings, covert insertion, sniping and observing, intelligence gathering and advanced firearm instruction for shooting from a moving vehicle. By all outside appearances, the training is classic counter-terrorist fare. Yet this tactical instruction isn't meant for Israel's terrorist enemies. This counter-terrorist instruction targets criminals. There is a new and innovative world in Israeli policing, spearheaded by the elite Border Guards, and new rules are being written in a land where law enforcement issues were once dominated by battling the world's deadliest enemies.

With the start of the new millenium, Israel is a land that is caught in a law and order transition. From 1997 up till the outbreak of fighting in Gaza and the West Bank in September 2000, the days of Israel's primary domestic internal security concern stemming from terrorists are over. While Israel is still engaged in a brutal war against Hamas and other fundamentalist Islamic guerrilla factions, Israeli citizens have now learned to fear robbery, rape and murder almost as much as they have suicide-bombings and hijackings. Crime in Israel, once an unheard of phenomenon, is now skyrocketing to European and even American statistics. According to officials statistics, murders, robberies, rapes, car-theft and other crimes, especially violent incidents, are up by as much as fifty-percent. In a nation where homicides were virtually nonexistent, homicide rates are now skyrocketing to European and even, in some cases, American per capita levels. The peace process that helped to establish marked terrain and a new future for Israelis and Palestinians has also created

During tactical training, Barak *unit officers undergo fire-malfunction-fire drills with the Jericho 941s. Firearm proficiency is a religion inside the Border Guards—especially with the force's elite special operations units. (Courtesy: Ma'Gav—Yechidat Barak)*

Barak *officers assemble in their Border Guard Class-As at a police ceremony honoring all those officers who have lost their lives in the line of duty. As can be seen by the badges on the tunics of many of these officers,* Barak*'s cops come from the elite of the Border Guard order of battle—from the Ya'ma'm to the undercover squads. (Courtesy: Ma'Gav—Yechidat Barak)*

new criminal boundaries. The territories under the control of the Palestinian Authority are safe havens for scores of stolen cars that are often used by Arafat's cops. The territories provide extradition-proof shelters to thieves, rapists, murderers and terrorists who operate freely on Israeli soil and are then protected by the Palestinian authorities. The influx of over one million immigrants from the former Soviet Union has also brought with it the Georgian, Ukrainian and Uzbeki Mafia. It brought contract killers, narcotics, protection, money laundering and an explosive prostitution industry. It brought Israel into the real world.

The Israeli Police, a national force of just over 25,000 officers divided into five geographic district commands: Jerusalem, Northern, Central, Southern, and Tel Aviv (district commanders are directly responsible to the police commissioner at National Headquarters in Jerusalem). The five districts are divided into thirteen sub-districts that are divided into police stations and police precincts. An administrative and operational headquarters that parallels the organization of the central police headquarters in Jerusalem manages each of the districts and sub-districts. Police functions such as investigations, operations, patrol, personnel management, and deployment of the Civil Guard, is carried out at various levels: national, district, sub-district, and station. The Border Guard, however, is organized in a different manner and has separate bases and its own unique line of command. The Border Guard, or Ma'Gav as it is known by its Hebrew-acronym, is a special paramilitary force of the Israel National Police, tasked with maintaining internal security and public order and provides assistance, when necessary, to regular operational police units in the fight against crime. Deployed throughout Israel, as well as in the West Bank and, now, the areas around Gaza, the Border Guard is unique in terms of its composition, with its officers including representatives of all Israel's ethnic groups: Jews, Druze, Circassians, Bedouins, Christians, and Moslems. Eighteen-year-old conscripts can do their mandatory military duty with the Border Guard instead of with the IDF. The Border Guards also field several "elite" counter-terrorist forces, including the *Ya'ma'm*, the national police counter-terrorist and hostage-rescue team, and the *Ya'mas*, an undercover tactical team that operates inside the West Bank mainly against Hamas and other terrorist factions.

The distinction between the regular police, or "blue police" as they are known in Israel, and the Border Guards, or "green police," had always been clear-cut. The blue cops handled traffic and crime and other matters related to internal security, and the Border Guards handled the territories,

Barak *prides itself as a unit that is a plain-clothes and undercover tactical squad—capable of blending in to specific geographies and city scenarios without ever being detected by the bad guy, while at the same time ready to respond to any situation—anytime—with heavy weapons at the ready. One of the unit's primary tools in this dual role is the motorcycle—it is fast, convenient and ideal for Tel Aviv's traffic-clogged streets. Here, during stake-out/assault training, an explosive charge is used as a "large-scale" stun device, allowing a* Barak *motorcycle to break out of an Observation Post and begin its charge toward a targeted location. (Courtesy: Ma'Gav—Yechidat Barak)*

Buses, whether they have been targeted by hijackers or by suicide-bombers, are very sensitive targets in Israel. Although military and police counter-terrorist units stand at the ready to respond to any terrorist incident inside the country, the Border Guard was determined to have their tactical anti-crime units capable to become first responders to be on site, at the ready, should an incident escalate and require immediate intervention. That capability, coupled with Israel's increasing crime problem, provides the Border Guard anti-crime teams with the tools to respond to a bus held by gun-wielding robbers, or an emotionally disturbed person (EDP). Here during bus-assault exercises in the Tel Aviv area, Barak officers use their motorcycles as convenient platforms from which to assault the besieged bus. (Courtesy: Ma'Gav—Yechidat Barak)

After unmarked Barak vehicles block the hijacked bus, the responders climb atop their motorbikes to obtain advantageous firing positions from where they can train their Jericho 941s on the perpetrators. The art of assaulting a seized bus is a dynamic process of split-second reflexes, perfected by months of grueling backbreaking instruction. Here, a Barak training officer observes the choreographed assault, searching for anything that can be improved on. (Courtesy: Ma'Gav—Yechidat Barak)

the Arab portions of Galilee and the agricultural belts. Yet as the Border Guards began to encounter serious narcotics and criminal activities in their sectors, and the blue police began to take a greater role in the counter-terrorist campaign, especially during the wave of suicide bombings that plagued the country from 1994 to 1997, the distinction between the two separate arms of the police blurred. When the rise in serious and violent crime began to baffle blue police officials, it was the Border Guards who would come to the rescue.

The thinking at Border Guard HQ was to provide the five police districts with elite tactical anti-crime teams that could be pressed into service for problem areas. The units would operate in both plain clothes and in uniform, and fulfil a function similar to the officers of the NYPD's Street Crime Unit, and the LAPD's Metropolitan Division. Yet because Border Guard units were better trained tactically than most regular police units, these new anti-crime teams would also serve as an on-call SWAT force. They would be capable of handling difficult scenarios that the blue police might not be able to handle, but which might not warrant the services of the *Ya'ma'm*, as well as serving as "first-responders" to major incidents and control the perimeter until the *Ya'ma'm's* arrival. The five district units were "*Alon*," in the North; "*Tzabar*" in the Central; "*Lavi*" in Jerusalem; "*Rotem*" in the South; and, "*Barak*" in Tel Aviv. These units would rewrite the way Israelis fought crime. Of the five district units, Barak is the youngest. It was created in January 1999 and tasked with serving Israel's most populated district, covering nearly one-third of the total national census. With their area of responsibility including Tel Aviv, the mixed town of Jaffa, Holon, Bat Yam, and the surrounding suburbs, Barak was in the epicenter of Israel's economic, residential and criminal soul. Barak would have its work cut out for itself.

When the Border Guard hierarchy created its tactical anti-crime teams, it did so realizing that the force possessed a unique talent pool of veteran counter-terrorists and undercover operatives who had literally rewritten the manual when it came to battling an unforgiving and violent enemy. Fighting criminals, Border Guard commanders theorized, was a lot like fighting terrorists—it required intelligence, initiative, innovation and guile. Veteran *Ya'ma'm* and *Ya'mas* officers who had come eyeball-to-eyeball with suicide bombers and masked gunmen could certainly translate the tactics and skills into a daily war against crime. Those tactics

A window, whether it be in a house or on a bus, is an opening, and during tubular assaults, is an access point that should be taken advantage of. Here, during bus assault exercises, four Barak officers use the open windows on a "hijacked" bus as firing ports to cover the assault force. (Courtesy: Ma'Gav—Yechidat Barak)

Anchoring his weight and balance with his left hand a Barak officer trains his 9mm Jericho 941 on a perpetrator. Note the female officer to his left. Barak is an egalitarian force, where female officers execute both tactical and undercover assignments alongside their male counterparts. (Courtesy: Ma'Gav—Yechidat Barak)

As Israel's crime problem begins to rival the terrorist threat as a national security issue of tremendous concern, police officers must learn to deal with scenarios where ordinary street thugs will hold hostages and barricade themselves inside homes and business. Here, during outdoor "shooting house" exercise, Barak officers train on rescuing hostages seized inside a restaurant setting during a robbery gone bad. (Courtesy: Ma'Gav—Yechidat Barak)

Although Border Guard regional anti-crime units pride themselves on their plain-clothes and undercover skills, especially in the apprehension of violent crime gangs wary of a police presence, the unit is a full-fledged tactical force that takes part in its fair share of high-risk arrest warrants and searches. Here, during a tactical search in the old part of Jaffa, an uniformed Barak officer uses the shoulder of a comrade as a firing platform.

Barak officers learn from their first hours in the unit to the dangerous explosive moments of a high-risk arrest warrant, that the unit operates as a team, and teamwork, as well as innovative tactics and weapons and safety proficiency, guarantees success on the street.

have become part of the battle plan for the streets of Tel Aviv and Superintendent K.,* Barak's commander, is just the man who can achieve the required results in this new form of Middle Eastern warfare.

Superintendent K. is a man who defines charisma. He is a warm and jovial officer, with a wry sense of humor and who commands tremendous respect among his cops. An idealist in an age of cynics, he commands a force of eighty men and women who are expected to perform above and beyond the call of duty in the military-like campaign of stopping murderers, rapists, drug dealers and even terrorists. K.'s special operations resume is impressive. A veteran of several of the Border Guards elite counter-terrorist entities, K.'s calling came in the ranks of the Ya'mas where he engaged Hamas suicide squads in a desperate war of survival in Gaza and the West Bank. "Being a good undercover operative didn't make you a case," K. recalls, "it kept you alive."

* Identity withheld for security reasons.

The Jericho 941 is a classic Israeli design—compact, economic, and based on combat requirements. The weapon is standard issue to all Israeli police officers.

Perspiring under the heavy fatigues and black balaclava, a Barak officer takes aim with his Mini-Uzi, as he endures the dangers of an unsecured corner and the 100° heat of Tel Aviv in the summer.

During house-clearing exercises near Tel Aviv, a Barak officer carefully peers around a corner before the rest of his compliment advances forward. The unit's primary close-quarter weapon is the Mini-Uzi 9mm submachine gun. Compact, robust, and indigenous, it is ideal for undercover operations as well as tubular assaults. Unlike many other tactical units in the world and unlike their counterparts in the Ya'ma'm, Border Guard tactical anti-crime teams prefer speed and firepower to heavy protective gear. The unit does not deploy heavy vests and body bunkers on most assignments.

In forming and nurturing the newly formed unit, K. surrounded himself with other veteran officers in the Border Guard's special operations order of battle. *Barak* boasts veterans from the *Ya'ma'm* in *Barak's* command cadre, as well as former comrades from the *Ya'mas*. From unit commander to the unit's operations and intelligence chiefs, each veteran cop has earned his stripes in the thankless and brutal terrorist battles that Israel has fought in the last decade. Those battles were won by innovation and tactical superiority—the cops won because they were smarter, faster, better equipped, better trained and quicker on the trigger than their terrorist foes. Applying that strategy toward Israel's war on crime, especially a campaign waged inside Israel's largest city and suburbs, was not an easy transition to make. After all, catching a murderous Hamas gang was not the same thing as snaring a car theft ring. Yet with a burgeoning crime rate and a growing organized crime influence, Border Guard veteran officers like K. realized that the war on crime would require the mindset and prowess of a special operations force.

Barak is composed of eighty veteran and career cops, as well as eighteen-year-old conscripts serving in the Border Guards as part of their three years of mandatory military service. The unit is tasked with being a little bit of everything—undercover force, detective squad and SWAT team—that can operate in problematic areas, or on problematic cases and trends, for the district command. The unit is tasked with saturating high-

The business end of a Barak *officer's Jericho 941 can be a daunting sight to anyone—especially considering the fact that unit personnel qualify frequently and with top scores on the range. Note the Border Guard patch worn on the officer's left sleeve.*

The compact size and unique style of the Mini-Uzi makes it an ideal weapon for the confined spaces for room clearing and tubular assaults. Although Israeli operators who have traveled abroad to visit similar units are obviously enamored with the MP5 family of 9mm submachine guns, the Mini-Uzi remains a reliable and capable sub-gun in the hands of Israeli police special operations teams.

crime areas, or residential and tourist areas that have been targeted by criminals, with both a plain-clothes and uniformed presence. The plain-clothed operatives will often conduct surveillance of a particular street or building with officers dressed in a wide-variety of disguises. Once the crime goes down, or once a suspect has been identified, the unit operatives put on their identifying blue and white Israeli Police baseball caps (Israeli police do not wear badges as do their counterparts in the United States or parts of Europe) and race into action. Because the Border Guards recruits from the entire spectrum of Israeli society, from tenth generation natives to new immigrants from the former Soviet Union, Ethiopia and the United States, their talent pool of cops can easily blend into any role, any ethnic neighborhood and any setting. *Barak* boasts officers who speak several dozen dialects of Russian languages, cops who can speak Arabic like a West Bank or Gaza native, as well as officers who can talk with authentic American accents and play the role of tourists. "In one instance," boasts K., "we were after a Uzbeki drug ring in Jaffa that the blue police had tried to crush for years. We had a young cop here who spoke the language with the proper dialect and we were able to secrete him into the neighborhood, and then into the clan, in a matter of weeks. In less than a month, we succeeded in shutting down a major narcotics operation all because we had the means to become one of them and infiltrate them." Once the proper evidence had been gathered against the targeted drug gang, *Barak* officers in full tactical kit raided their fortified and heavily defended location.

Barak is also tasked with assembling evidence in ongoing investigations. As a throwback to many Border Guard operations against Hamas in Gaza and the West Bank, *Barak* officers are experts in the art of covert surveillance. The unit is equipped with a wide assortment of surveillance and intelligence-gathering equipment, from long-range observation cameras to night-vision. The ability to set up camouflaged observation posts in both an urban and rural setting, a skill mastered in the Occupied Territories, has allowed *Barak* to make some 400 high-profile arrests in the one year that the unit has been operational. They have closed down dozens of drug dens and narcotics rings, and they have seriously clamped down on low level criminal activity in parts of the district where thugs once ruled the day. Most surveillance operations are carried out by what the unit called "Special Operations Teams," that can stakeout locations, gather intelligence on an ongoing criminal enterprise, and even affect and arrest. Many Special Operations Team deployments are supported by the unit marksmen and observers who provide tactical and counter-sniper backup to many sensitive police operations.

As a mobile tactical force, the Border Guard anti-crime units are full-fledged SWAT teams capable of executing high-risk search and arrest warrants, as well as providing chase to heavily armed felons pursued by the police. *Barak*, whose officers are equipped with Jericho 941s and Mini-Uzis, as well as M16 assault rifles, are proficient in both covert and dynamic entries. Unit officers also routinely train in live-fire exercises

The personal kit of a Barak officer is meant to be light, comfortable, and suitable for close-quarters and hot weather. Most of Barak's *operations take place in an undercover and plain-clothes setting, where the assault vest and extra firepower must be camouflaged underneath civilian dress.*

Israeli criminals, especially Arab gangs and those belonging to organized crime elements from the former Soviet Union, have begun to resist the police more and more in recent years. In a sight once thought as never-to-be-seen in the Jewish State, police are carrying out routine warrants against locations in residential Israeli cities with the tactics and tools once reserved for counter-terrorist operations. Here, in Jaffa, a Barak *officer secures a corner of a staircase during a drug raid.*

from moving automobiles, as well as from motorcycles, in order to stop fleeing criminals or terrorists who attempt to break through fortified roadblocks and traffic stops.

When the Border Guard tactical anti-crime units were created, senior police officials were interested in creating a SWAT-type unit that could do more than execute high-risk arrest warrants. In case a terrorist, or even a heavily-armed criminal or emotionally disturbed individual, seized hostages anywhere in the country, Border Guard commanders wanted to be able to have their district tactical anti-crime teams capable of being first responders. Although the Ya'ma'm and Israeli military hostage-rescue forces are centrally located and can respond to a crisis in haste, police officials wanted to have the luxury of fielding a force of officers who could respond tactically and dynamically to a hostage situation gone bad—be it a terrorist holding a bus full of passengers at gunpoint, or a robbery of restaurant that turned into a standoff.

The Border Guard anti-crime tactical teams routinely train in all facets of tubular assaults, dynamic entries, and hostage-rescue. In one training scenario that was recently honed at the Border Guard training facility at Beit Horon, a two-story building had been seized by terrorists threatening to kill all their hostages if their demands were not immediately met. When gunfire erupted from inside the location, the officers moved in for the dynamic assault. As several officers carried a ladder to a second-story window, the first-floor assault force moved in for the attack. The front door of the location was blown off its hinges and the officers moved in the precise and expedient choreography of the room clear—each terrorist target was quickly sliced down by accurate bursts of 9mm fire. On the second floor, the officers made entry courtesy of their ladder and proceeded to eliminate the terrorist threats with their Jerichos and Mini-Uzis.

One of *Barak's* hostage-rescue specialties is bus assaults. The Tel Aviv area is *the* Israeli metropolis and without trams or true rail service, buses are the lifeblood of the city. It is because of their importance that terrorists have routinely targeted buses so many times in the past. Yet buses are difficult targets to assault. Windows and doors make it difficult for the surrounding police forces to make any surprise assaults without the terrorists possibly having the time to begin executing the hostages. In order to increase their chances of seizing the initiative and gaining the element of surprise, *Barak* officers train to assault hijacked buses in civilian clothes, utilizing the speed and mobility of their motorcycles. In exercises that the unit routinely carries out, several squads of *Barak* officers on motorcycle assault the surrounded bus. Getting to a besieged bus on motorcycle is faster than by racing to it on foot, and the motorcycles provide the officers with a convenient platform on which to stand when aiming their weapons at the inside of the bus.

Teamwork on a tactical raid is an essential element to officer survival—especially when the bad guys are often armed with ordnance stolen from the IDF! Here, inside the squalor of a Jaffa tenement, officers cover one another as they head up a flight of stairs in a methodological manner, toward the targeted rooftop apartment.

The sun is about to set into the Mediterranean and the hotels and bathers along Tel Aviv's beaches are basked in one last warming wave of orange light. As the lazy day of August comes to an end, and the city slowly winds down to a stalled pace of after-work fun and routine, the rear area of a police station in Jaffa is abuzz with activity. Inside a frenetic office where the pushed-to-capacity air conditioner stifles the room with an ear-splitting buzzing noise, a half dozen *Barak* officers scramble on telephones as they coordinate three ongoing investigations, two ongoing surveillance operations, and a drug raid planned for the evening. Superintendent K. juggles a cellular phone in on hand, and calls on two land lines in the order dealing with a roving surveillance of an informant who is going to lead officers to an extortion ring, as well as a buy-and-bust operation at a heroin stash house near Jaffa. On two other lines, K. handles a call from headquarters in Jerusalem concerning developments in the ongoing and baffling case of the serial Tel Aviv rapist, as well as with a logistics officer at Lod concerning vehicle repair. K. has been at the office for nearly twelve hours this balmy August Thursday, and his day hasn't really started.

As a purple dusk descends over Tel Aviv, and the drug raid's H-Hour nears, some twenty-five *Barak* officers have gathered for K.'s inspection. A dozen Border Guard officers, conscripts wearing their green fatigues, display their Kevlar helmets and undergo the mandatory weapons inspection. Other unit members, seasoned veterans who'll operate in plain clothes, present their masquerades and coordinate radio frequencies. For good measure, a marksman carrying an M4 Carbine with a scope loads his gear into the unit's high-tech surveillance van. Several officers, Mini-Uzis tucked conveniently into their leather jackets, rev up the engines on their Kawasaki racers, as they prepare to head to the targeted location to cut off the escape of any perpetrators attempting to flee the *Barak* dragnet. Two officers hone their American accents as they prepare to play the role of two lost tourists and occupy a lookout.

To K., the seriousness of the preparation and detailed planning reminds him of his days in Gaza, Ramallah and Nablus. Yet as Israel looks at the new threats it faces in the next century, the distinction between the war against terrorism and the war against serious and violent criminals is blurred. Both terrorists and criminals endanger the very fabric of security in Israeli society and if both are to be defeated it will require tactical precision and ingenious innovation—something that Israelis are quite good at.

Excellent close-up view of the kit carried by a "uniformed" Barak officer into battle.

Excellent close-up view of the rear of the assault load bearing vest worn on all uniformed Barak operations.

Poised to take down anyone foolish enough to resist, a Barak officer moves in on a suspect while training the sights of his Jericho 941 on the perpetrator's head.

Windows are convenient openings, especially evening when they are barred and sealed shut. During a drug raid in Jaffa, a Barak officer covers a group of suspects through the window bars of a small first-floor apartment.

Parked behind the Jaffa Police Station, with the Mediterranean and the Tel Aviv skyline in the background, a marked Barak Land Cruiser is prepared for a night of patrolling and surveillance.

The choreography of a Barak plain-clothes car takedown. Elements of the roadblock force block the advance and retreat of the targeted vehicle. Plain-clothes officers, identifiable by their blue baseball caps with "police" emblazoned across the sides in both Hebrew and English, leap out of the stakeout cars and swarm the targeted vehicle. As can be seen in this photo, the use of female officers can be a distraction to the criminals. They are more likely to be on the lookout for a muscular male who might be a cop, but not as suspecting of a beautiful buxom woman who carries a Jericho 941 in her back and just happens to be one of the Border Guards "Finest."

Arafat's Veil of Armor

The PA's Presidential Security Apparatus

Samuel M. Katz

Following morning prayers inside a Ramallah mosque, senior agents of the Presidential Security Guard escort President Arafat to his armored Mercedes sedan. (Courtesy: Steve Hartov)

On a warm and dusty day near Amman, the capital of Jordan, the motorcade of silver Mercedes sedans and white Chevy Suburbans, Mitsubishi Pajeros and Land Rovers, pushed the limits of the wide open roads, heading west toward the Jordan River and the West Bank. The vehicles, all sporting Palestinian flags, raced through the wind and the 100º-in-the-shade heat, in a fast moving armada of lead cars, principal vehicles, and follow cars. The heavily armed agents standing precariously on sideboards welded to the sides of the Suburbans, were uncomfortable in their Ramallah-purchased suits and ties. Remaining alert while remaining on board the fast-moving all-terrain vehicle was difficult, as was squinting through the blinding sun to scan the horizon for any signs of an ambush, a roadside bomb, or a sniper's perch. Suddenly, an agent standing outside one of the Land Rovers shouted RPG over a Motorola radio system worn on his belt, as four figures running down a small sand dune near an intersection were seen aiming rocket propelled grenades and automatic weapons. In an instant, a motorcade of unified movement and force dissipated into a myriad of swirling countermoves. As a lead vehicle and the principal's armored Mercedes executed picture-perfect J-turns to escape and evade the inevitable gauntlet of fire, two follow cars loaded to capacity with heavily armed agents raced toward the attackers. The security agents veered their vehicles into parallel positions in front of the attackers to deflect any attack away from the principal onto the counterassault team. Removing 9mm automatics and AK-47s from their vehicles, the agents launched a furious fusillade of automatic fire at the

Not the safest way to ride around at high-speeds, but certainly effective in needing to respond dynamically to any possible assassination threat. In Ramallah, Presidential Security agents rode on the sideboards of their Jeep Cherokee follow car.

The agents of Presidential Security are heavily armed and loyal to the core. Here, inside the Muqata*, a team of agents riding on the sideboards of a Jeep Cherokee Loredo give a scrutinizing once over to a French TV cameraman covering President Arafat.*

Under a veil of human security that has dedicated its life to protecting the president, Yasir Arafat is driven to his compound in Ramallah in his armored Mercedes sedan.

Presidential Security commanders confer about an upcoming move outside of Ramallah.

attackers, not relenting in their barrage until the threat had been destroyed. On a nearby hilltop, a man wearing neatly pressed olive fatigues and smoking a Marlboro uttered a few, yet approving, words over a Motorola walkie-talkie. The Jordanian special operations instructor supervising the training also looked pleased. These men, the instructor noted, were ready for anything.

For nearly forty years, the men who protected PLO Chairman Yasir Arafat had, indeed, been ready for anything. They had fought brutal wars against the Israelis, the Jordanians, the Lebanese Army, the Lebanese Christians, the Syrians, the Druze, and among themselves. They had perpetrated hundreds of terrorist attacks in the Middle East, in Europe and even Asia, and had become masters at guerrilla warfare. Yet on September 13, 1993, when President Bill Clinton prodded PLO Chairman Yasir Arafat and Israeli Prime Minister Yitzhak Rabin to shake hands on the White House lawn, the Palestinian Praetorian Guard would forever be transformed from rogues to legitimate representatives. The men who protected Yasir Arafat and the very stability of the about-to-be-created Palestinian Authority in the Gaza Strip and portions of the West Bank would, by the very nature of their mission, be transformed from perpetrators to protectors of the peace process. And, for the men tasked with executing this now sacrosanct role, the stakes would be enormous.

For years, dignitary protection and special operations in the ranks of the PLO were the domain of Force 17—a mysterious force of bodyguards and commandos tasked with safeguarding key Palestinian VIPs as well as executing "special" missions against Israel. The men and, indeed, women who were selected to join the ranks of the force were all volunteers who had been offered the chance to serve the revolution due to their intelligence, courage, dedication and, most importantly, loyalty. Many Force 17 operatives were trained in the Beka'a Valley in numerous guerrilla camps, as well as in Warsaw Pact facilities run by Soviet, Polish, Czech, Hungarian and East German special forces, and intelligence services. For a service designed to protect one of the most targeted individuals in the world, Force 17's protective ethic was a simple belief that "deterrence, intelligence and firepower would negate all threats." In Lebanon, where Arafat's PLO was headquartered, as well as in other Arab capitals, any individual or group that was believed to threaten the PLO Chairman was dealt with harshly.

Yet the signing of the Israeli-Palestinian Peace Accords and the return of Arafat to the Gaza Strip in 1994 transformed the PLO and its military and security forces had to shed their guerrilla past and conventionalize their roles, their methods, their tools, and their mission.

The emblem of the Presidential Guard unit, emblazoned on all detail vehicles.

A senior Presidential Guard mans a post armed with years of experience and a trusted AK-47 7.62mm assault rifle.

One of the many armored Suburbans used by Presidential Security agents on motorcades.

One of the many Land Rover all-terrain vehicles used by agents of the Presidential Security.

Palestinian security and intelligence forces would now have to fit the well-defined scope and order of battle that were clearly spelled out in the Oslo Peace Accords. These forces, some trained by the Libyans, North Koreans, Syrians and Bulgarians, would now have to operate and cooperate with their former adversaries in the Israeli Shin Bet, the American CIA, as well as the French, British and German federal law enforcement agencies.

For Arafat's dignitary protection detail, the transformation would be all encompassing. Firstly, the title of Force 17—something that the Israelis objected to strongly—was officially changed to "Palestinian Presidential Security." Agents in the newly renamed force were suddenly to be shed their guerrilla mission, and assume a dignitary protection role like the U.S. Secret Service, U.S. State Department Diplomatic Security Service and Britain's Scotland Yard, and they needed urgent refresher training. Many inside Palestinian Presidential Security were sent to immediate training in Jordan and Egypt, as well instruction with the French *Groupe de Sécurité de Président de la République* (GSPR), considered by many to be the most experienced and most professional dignitary protection service in Europe. In the force's new training regimen, great emphasis was placed on identifying and diminishing a threat to their principal *before* that threat would have a chance to act. Firepower was no longer an indiscriminate series of magazine-emptying barrages meant to destroy a target—and every living thing around it. Once a weapon was produced and a trigger pulled, the firepower needed to be brief and accurate. It was not an agent's job to battle it out with a terrorist force in the protracted brutal battles that were once waged in Beirut. Rather, removing the principal from harm's way became the absolute primary objective. "Better to live to fight another day and hunt the Tangos down tomorrow," according to one senior U.S. dignitary protection expert involved in the Palestinian retraining, "than to bury your leader and suffer from all-out civil war."

The complexities of the Middle East, and the Arab-Israeli conflict in particular, provide Palestinian Presidential Security with tremendous work challenges. With the Palestinian Authority literally split geographically between the Gaza Strip and cities and villages in the West Bank, Palestinian Authority President Arafat splits his time between his government offices in Gaza and his West Bank headquarters in Ramallah, some fifteen kilometers north of Jerusalem. Both Gaza and the West Bank present enormous and varied threats to the various Palestinian security services. In Gaza, where Islamic fundamentalism is strong, Hamas and the Islamic Jihad are powerful and heavily armed fanatical foes of the peace process. In numerous clashes with the Palestinian police and

During Secretary of State Albright's December 1999 visit to the Muqata, a Presidential Security platoon leader assembles his men into line.

Palestinian Presidential Security agents help to escort and protect Secretary of State Madeleine K. Albright during her visit to President Arafat's compound in Ramallah in December 1999.

With his finger never far from the trigger of his trusted AK-47, a Presidential Security captain watches agents in his detail as they secure a portion of the presidential compound in Ramallah.

security forces, they have displayed their brutal resolve to end the rapprochement between Arafat and the Israelis, and bring about an Islamic State in Palestine through a Jihad, or holy war. In the West Bank, where Hamas and the Islamic Jihad are also strong, many Palestinian security sources fear the right-wing Israeli settlers as their primary threat. After all, it was a right-wing Israeli who, on November 4, 1995, assassinated Prime Minister Yitzhak Rabin and, for some three years, placed a mortal gunshot wound to the peace process.

Although a newly formed land passage now connects Gaza and the West Bank, much of Arafat's movements in the territories, especially from the two seats of power, are controlled by the Israelis, this is especially true following the outbreak of the September Intifadah. Arafat makes all of his moves from Ramallah to Gaza in one of the two Russian-

A senior Presidential Security officer moves quickly amid a sea of U.S. Department of State Diplomatic Security Service agents securing the Muqata during Secretary of State Albright's visit with President Arafat.

built Mi-8 choppers, as well as brief flights to Amman. Longer presidential flights, to cities like Cairo or Tunisia, or even to European capitals and even the United States, once made in a Saudi Gulfstream on loan to the Palestinian Authority are now made on a presidential jet. Any move by President Arafat, whether it be a trip to Bethlehem or a state visit to Brussels and the European Union, is preceded by an advance vanguard of Presidential Security agents who meet and coordinate security concerns with their local counterparts. Overseas, such as in Belgium where the elite ESI counter-terrorist team augments security arrangements for Arafat visits, to the United States, where the tactical operators from the U.S. Department of State Diplomatic Security Service's Mobile Security Division enhance security provisions, agents from Presidential Security maintain that final cohesive and secure inner perimeter around the president.

Inside the Palestinian Authority, any move by President Arafat to a mosque, city center or other cultural gathering is preceded by agents from one of the nearly dozen other security services (see below). These forces saturate the motorcade routes, address known or possible threats, and augment the local police force and their rapid response teams, SWAT-like forces tasked to tactically deal with threats and terrorist attacks. Presidential Security motorcade packages consist of snake-long convoys of vehicles, follow cars and emergency medical vehicles that are all poised, at a radio signal, to swing into action. Such security packages are also put into place whenever a visiting dignitary, from Israeli Prime Minister Ehud Barak, to former Russian President Boris Yelstin, to

Following the successful conclusion of their bilateral negotiations, Secretary of State Albright and President Arafat share the podium for a press conference under the watchful eyes of the Diplomatic Security Service and the Palestinian Presidential Security.

As Secretary of State Albright and President Arafat address an assembly of cameras and reporters, a no-nonsense captain from Presidential Security keeps an eye on the press.

Members of the Bethlehem Police rapid response team stand at the ready moments before the arrival of a high-level presidential motorcade.

President Bill Clinton and Secretary of State Madeleine K. Albright.

It is a blustery cold night in December outside the *Muqata,* President Arafat's Ramallah compound, and the security blanket thrown over the fortress-like installation is all encompassing and nerves are at a fever's pitch. As the sounds of gunfire is heard in the distance near an Israeli settlement, a Presidential Security captain wearing camouflaged fatigues and clutching a weathered AK-47 barks a series of orders at agents, also in uniform, at the gate to the sprawling facility. Sharpshooters peer through night vision scopes atop the *Muqata* and alongside the many homes that surround the Palestinian West Bank White House. All weapons are locked and loaded. The Presidential Security force is joined this frigid night by agents from the U.S. Department of State's Diplomatic Security Service assigned to Secretary of State Albright's detail. The U.S. Secretary of State, in the region to kick-start the stagnant peace talks, will be spending the evening at the *Muqata,* following day long negotiations in Jerusalem with Israeli leaders. Fundamentalist forces on both sides of the religious fence have vowed to end the process with a furious flurry of violence. Few inside the *Muqata* take the threat lightly.

For the men of the Presidential Security detail that evening in Ramallah, as well as those serving in Gaza, the irrefutable fact that they are the protectors of the changing face of the Palestinian people is entrenched in their mission. They realize that murder and assassination is part and parcel with the Middle East and that, in the course of protecting their president, they might be forced to lay down their lives, so that the dream of peace can continue. Yet they also realize that their battle experience and more conventional training has turned them into a highly cohesive force, capable of terminating any terrorist enemy with unforgiving firepower.

Police Special Forces teams, in their black fatigues and green Kevlar vests, prepare to join advance plain-clothes agents from the Presidential Security in aggressive patrols throughout the motorcade route into Bethlehem.

Police special forces help secure the area around the Church of the Nativity in Bethlehem prior to a visit by President Arafat.

A Presidential Security GMC Suburban blocks the entrance to the Church of the Nativity prior to the arrival of the presidential motorcade.

A Bethlehem police officer scans the crowd of onlookers and tourists just moments before the arrival of the presidential motorcade and package. Communications between the lead Presidential Security teams and the local police officers in the field is excellent.

Palestinian Police, Security and Intelligence Forces

The Agreement on the Gaza Strip and Jericho Area of 4 May 1994 and the Oslo II Agreement of 1996 stress the need for a "strong police force". Annex I, Article IV(2) of the Oslo II Agreement of 1995 states that the Palestinian Police shall consist of one integral unit under the control of the Council, composed of four branches: the Civil Police, Public Security, Preventive Security, Intelligence and Emergency Services and Rescue. "In each district, all members of the four Police branches shall be subordinate to one central command." At least 10 different police or security forces operate within and, on occasion, outside the areas under the jurisdiction of the Palestinian Authority. Each Palestinian district may have several security branches operating alongside one another. No security force appears to be subject to any civilian control although in theory the governor (*muhafez*) of each town has overall authority over the forces in his area. The extent of control of the leaders of each security force over units stationed in other parts of the West Bank is also unclear. The Palestinian police force was recruited partly from Palestinians from the Diaspora, including members of the Palestinian Liberation Army, the armed force of the PLO, and partly from local people from the West Bank and Gaza Strip. Originally composed of 12,000 police, by July 1995 its number had risen to 20,000 and by September 1996 there were believed to be more than 40,000 police in different branches of the security forces. In the Gaza Strip, with about 20,000 police, there is one law enforcement officer for every 50 people, possibly the highest ratio of police to civil population in the world.

Armed with a variety of 9mm handguns (SIG-Sauers, Brownings and even Glocks) as well as AK-47 assault rifles, a Presidential Security follow car races behind the motorcade ready to respond to any terrorist attack on the life of the principal. (Courtesy: Steve Hartov)

A senior Presidential Guard officer stands in front of one of President Arafat's two Mi-8 choppers at a landing zone at the Muqata.

One of the President Arafat's two aging Russian-built Mi-8 helicopters ready for take-off.

Wings of Angels Over Skies Of Fire

Unit 669: The Israel Air Force's Aeromedical Evacuation Unit

Samuel M. Katz

An Unit 669 CH-53 Yasur *moves about the snow capped peaks of Mt. Hermon, atop the Golan Heights, during cold-weather exercises, with two operators in tow.* (Biton Heyl Ha'Avir)

"Remember—the pilot is all alone out there. He has in his head three years and millions of dollars of training, and some of the country's most important secrets. He has a wife, two kids, and parents who love and need him. He could be your friend, your friend's friend, and he could be your neighbor. He is all alone out there. If captured, he will be beaten, humiliated and tortured beyond human endurance. He is likely to be executed. He is alone out there. You are his only hope!"

A Unit 669 commander to a group of operators prior to a mission inside Lebanon

IAF patch.

Unit 669 Wings.

On this January morning, the tranquil blue Mediterranean wasn't being true to its namesake. Instead of forming placid waves, the waters off the northern Israeli coast were choppy, stormy, and definitely not inviting to the crew of the IDF Navy Dabur, "Bee," patrol craft anchored in the tumultuous sea. As the Dabur's commander, a nervous first lieutenant, stood on the sea-swept deck and looked at his diver's watch, the pounding beat of a synchronized visitor was heard in the distance overhead. Moments later, a mammoth CH-53 "*Yasur,*" the IDF's name for the Sea Stallion workhorse, dreary in its mud-brown camouflage scheme, hovered above the small craft; its giant rotors created a powerful and disturbing whirlpool around the small boat.

Just as had been coordinated at headquarters, a "lucky" volunteer from the Dabur, wearing a wet suit and life vest, jumped into the choppy sea to, hopefully, be rescued. His plunge was the signal to the *Yasur* that two men, looking like spacemen from a B-movie in their bright orange wet suits and shiny white helmets, should be slowly lowered into the stormy waters. After checking the "wounded" sailor's medical condition in a well-rehearsed-though-fastidious manner, the visitors from above fastened the unfortunate volunteer into a stretcher attached to a specially designed winch, invented by Unit 669, that was capable of lifting up to 7,700 lb. and raised their gloved thumbs to the chopper pilot straight overhead—the signal that ordered the chopper crew, and whatever they happened to be carrying, up. Just as quickly as it had appeared, the *Yasur* departed for home.

Inside the helicopter, the sailor was "treated and stabilized" by a crew of medics, supervised by a flight surgeon. Though just executing a training endeavor, the helicopter crew attended to their duties with dire seriousness. The completion of this difficult exercise occurred when the *Yasur* touched down on the landing pad of Haifa's Ram'bam Hospital and the team commander, Major E., clicked his stopwatch - the smile on his face indicating a job well done.

The joint IDF Navy and IAF exercise was difficult and demanding for the IAF's Unit 669, which is the most professional, highly trained, integrated, and specialized unit in the IDF's impressive "commando" Order of Battle. It is an elite force of covert warriors and rescuers, specially tasked with the rescue of downed pilots, wounded soldiers, and anyone else in need trapped behind enemy lines. Many thankful IAF pilots, who owe their lives to the pilots, mechanics, commandos, medics, and doctors of Unit 669, have labeled them "the best of them all." Excellence in maneuvers is one thing—performing above-and-beyond the call of duty under fire is another world completely.

There was no need for map coordinates that night over southern Lebanon—the brilliance of the tracer rounds erupting in the darkness was all the illumination required to light up the landing zone. The fires of the Lebanese night looked daunting from atop the Mediterranean after midnight on of September 5, 1997, as did the cries for help bursting across the headsets of the helicopter pilots and rescue commandos and

An IAF F-15 flies patrol over southern Lebanon—the pilots secure in the knowledge that should they be shot down, Unit 669 will be right there to pick him up. (Biton Heyl Ha'Avir)

they eased the 10,000 lbs. of CH-53 transport chopper into a dive and a clearing of lemon trees that would be used as a landing strip. It had been a bad night for Israeli special forces in the bullet-scarred landscape of Southern Lebanon. A strike by naval commandos from Flotilla 13 against Hizbollah targets in the village of Ansariyah had ended with the pull of a trip wire and the destruction of a sixteen-man strike-team that fell square into the center of a terrorist ambush. Virtually all the naval commandos had been killed or critically wounded in the initial blast, and a small army of Hizbollah terrorists was now closing in for the kill. One miraculous survivor of the melee, the radioman, managed to wage a lone-wolf campaign of survival until the dead and wounded could be rescued by air. Time was running out, however. They needed a miracle.

In the Israel Defense Forces (IDF) order of battle, miracles are usually reserved for the medevac commandos of "Unit 669," the heliborne Israel Air Force (IAF) team tasked with the rescue and recovery of personnel trapped behind enemy lines—from F-16 pilots forced to eject to naval commandos trapped in an ambush. Upon the first call for help that bloody night in Lebanon, a flight of AH-1S Cobra helicopter gunships were scrambled from forward fields in northern Israel to rake the encroaching Hizbollah gunmen with cannon and guided-missile fire. Landing some 150 meters away from the fire-fight, the combined force of Flotilla 13 and Unit 669 operators raced out of the rear cargo door to assist in providing cover fire to the evacuation. While one force raced to the dead and wounded, others headed toward the battle to create a perimeter of defensive fire. The unit doctor raced between the wounded

At an evacuation center along the Lebanese coast, critically wounded Israeli soldiers are ferried to hospitals in northern Israel. (IDF Spokesman)

An Unit 669 operator picks up a wounded sailor from on board a Dabur patrol boat in the Mediterranean. (Biton Heyl Ha'Avir)

and the dying, in a tireless effort to save as many lives as he could. As the chopper took off, though, the doctor was cut down by small arms fire, launched by Hizbollah gunmen in a Mercedes sedan that pulled up close to the CH-53. An AH-1S Cobra responded by decimating the Mercedes—and its occupants—with a burst of cannon fire. For the next two hours, Unit 669 rescue force searched the area for bodies and body parts, abandoned classified equipment, and any wounded personnel that might have been left behind; there was fear among the rescuers that they were

Tel-Aviv—Jerusalem Highway, July 6, 1989. Unit 669 is called in to evacuate the victims of a terrorist attack on an inter-city bus. (Biton Heyl Ha'Avir)

Maidun, southern Lebanon. Under heavy Hizbollah fire, Unit 669 chopper evacuates wounded paratroopers from the battle-zone. (IDF Spokesman)

missing one body. As the rescuers searched, the secondary team established a perimeter to secure the operation. Although under heavy fire, the commandos managed to initiate suppressive cover fire of their own to hold the guerrillas at bay. IAF operations in support of the secondary search was non-stop. Flying in pairs, IAF attack choppers searched, identified, engaged a small legion of hostile forces that were waging a desperate battle of their own. At 04:30, two IAF UH-60 Blackhawks reached the LZ. The first chopper evacuated one wounded and one dead naval commando, bags containing body parts, as well as classified equipment that had been abandoned by the ambushed operators.

The following day, as the nation mourned the twelve dead commandos and as the units and their families buried their dead, Israeli President Ezer Weizman looked over the helicopters that participated in the daring rescue under fire. Examining the tail of one of the CH-53s, Weizman, himself a former fighter pilot and commander of the Israel Air Force, was awestruck by the gaping bullet holes. "The courage to fly into such a fusillade of enemy fire is incredible," one air force officer commented as the president stood amazed by the damage to the chopper, "the courage to land there is even greater!"

Almost every air force on earth deploys an elite, medically trained air rescue unit specifically tasked with the rescue of downed pilots. Combat pilots are extremely well trained, dangerously intimate with top-secret hardware and procedures, and often dispatched to wage a lone war against enemy targets far from the safety of friendly lines. For the *Heyl Ha'Avir*, the Hebrew name for the Israel Air Force (IAF) in its early years, however, long-range operations far from home were nothing more than imaginative visions of the future and, as a result, no specially trained airborne rescue force existed. The tragically outnumbered IAF could barely hold its own against the combined might of four Arab air forces; its skill and dedication were meant to defend Israeli skies rather than attack faraway Arab targets.

Acquisition of the Mirage, Vautour, and Super-Mystere, as well as the 1967 war, changed everything. Targets as far away as Iraq and Alexandria, in Egypt, were now well within the IAF's grasp, and the likelihood of a plane's, and pilot's, being downed in enemy territory became a reality. The IAF performed brilliantly in that war, however, and, in many cases, pilots shot down over enemy territory soon found themselves greeting the advanced vanguards of IDF armored divisions. The true marker that indicated the need to form an IAF air rescue force was the brutal War of Attrition-a turning point that transformed the IAF from a "very good" Third World air force to one capable of competing with the "super-power big boys." First, on October 21, 1967, came the opening salvo of the War of Attrition when the flagship of the IDF Navy, the destroyer I.N.S. *Eilat*, was attacked by a Egyptian patrol boats, which fired Soviet-built Styx sea-to-sea missiles, and sunk off the coast of Sinai. Many of the Eilat's 220 sailors were killed in the explosions and fires caused the missile volley; others were badly burned and in dire need of emergency medical care.

The IAF duly dispatched several Super Frelon helicopters to pick up the dead and wounded, often making gallant attempts to pluck them out of flaming waters amid the chaos of enemy fire and cries of anguish, but the Super Frelon crews were combat flyers, not rescuers or medics. As a result, the badly hurt had to be transported to a makeshift aid station on the Sinai shoreline for emergency care before being sent to a hospital back in Israel. Although 152 of the *Eilat* crew members were saved by the Super Frelon pilots, many have argued that the delay in bringing immediate medical attention contributed to the final death toll of forty-seven sailors. The sinking of the *Eilat* had numerous military, as well as political, repercussions. In IAF Headquarters the effective heliborne rescue began to play in the minds of some innovative operational planners who appreciated the need for a specially trained force of heliborne warriors and healers to be on call for such tragic eventualities.

But the sinking of the flagship was just one military reality of the full-scale bloodletting of the War of Attrition. Another reality was long-range aerial bombings of targets deep inside Egypt. When Soviet-produced and, toward the end of the three-year conflict, Soviet-manned

During time-trials for Unit 669 chopper pilots, a Bell-212 races along a Roman aqueduct along the Mediterranean coast. (Biton Heyl Ha'Avir)

Because of the IAF's global reach, as illustrated by the refueling capacity of an IAF F-15, Unit 669 has become one of the busiest commando-rescue units in the world. (Biton Heyl Ha'Avir)

surface-to-air missile batteries and radar-guided guns began to blast the IAF aerial bombers out of the sky, still another reality was the capture, killing, and wounding of pilots far beyond Israel's borders.

Although the creation of a specially trained air rescue force was an impossible task during wartime, dozens of pilots were eventually rescued by helicopter. One spectacular rescue occurred on June 30, 1970, when two F-4E Phantoms attacking an Egyptian SAM battery were shot down. In all, four chutes opened; the pilot and navigator from the first plane were captured, as was the pilot from the second plane. Only the navigator from the second Phantom managed to manipulate his chute away from the pursuing Egyptian forces and hails of AA fire launched at him (the Egyptians even fired a SA-2 surface-to-air missile at his descending chute) to reach tentative safety. His only hope for rescue was a small, though powerful, communications and homing device that faithfully transmitted a code back to his home base.

At night, when chances of a helicopter's succumbing to ground fire were minimal, a chopper was dispatched to bring the navigator, or his body, back to Israel. Flying blind, straight into the Egyptian Army's front-line position, was an act of great courage for the chopper's crew, but reaching the enemy's front line was the easiest third of the night's mission; they still had to find the pilot—his device had a range finder margin for error of 200 meters—retrieve him, and put it into gear for the "bumpy" hop back to Sinai. Captain T., the chopper's pilot, described the mission: "It was like finding an electronic needle in a haystack laying atop a time bomb, but some lucky flying and the navigator's courage allowed us to find him without too much difficulty. It was too dark for us to see him, however, and we couldn't have known that he had buried his flashlight with his gear after bailing out."

When the signal from the communications device came in as clear as it could transmit, but still nothing was spotted, Captain T. realized that he would never find the navigator in the pitch-black desert. Courageously, he decided to do what he had been strictly ordered not to back at base: illuminate the chopper's two projector lamps onto the desert hills below. The lights helped locate the appreciative navigator and, at first, surprised the Egyptians. Incessant AA fire soon followed, however, and only Captain T.'s zigzag evasive flight pattern allowed the chopper to escape the splintering glow of 30mm tracer fire and make it back home, even though dozens of bullet and shrapnel holes had peppered the aircraft. In Israel, Captain T. witnessed the reunion of the navigator with his expecting wife and thanked the Almighty for the reliability of his helicopter.

The advent of the transport chopper-the Super Frelon, the CH-53, and the Bell-205-into the IAF arsenal should have meant the formation of a special air rescue unit during the War of Attrition, but it didn't. A training accident involving the destruction of two Phantoms, and the IAF's subsequent and unprofessional rescue attempt in the Gulf of Aqaba, near the Red Sea resort town of Eilat, did, however. The incident gave birth to Unit 669. The outbreak of the 1973 Yom Kippur War delayed the formation of the unit by one year, even though countless dramatic helicopter rescues of downed pilots stranded behind enemy lines were executed during the conflict. Oddly enough, in 1974 when the IAF created Unit 669 (or, as it's known to the natives, *Yehidat Ha'Chilutz Shel Heyl Ha'Avir*, Hebrew for Aeromedical Evacuation Unit since the designation of "669" was classified for over twenty years) IAF commander was Major-General Benjamin "Benny" Peled, a flyer who, in the 1956 Sinai Campaign, was himself shot down by ground fire behind enemy lines and rescued by a Piper Cub.

When the *Heyl Ha'Avir* created Unit 669, IAF Headquarters was determined to produce something much more than a clone of one of the many reconnaissance commando units in the IDF's green, or army, inventory. It had to be a special forces unit in the truest definition of the word: combat proficient, cohesive, and able to reach and exit any enemy objective; a heliborne trauma center of well-trained doctors and medics able to administer the most sophisticated medical attention; and all-weather and on call twenty-four-hours-per-day, because pilots are shot down, soldiers are wounded in a fire-fight, and civilian accidents occur without prior notification.

To form such a unit, Unit 669 had to produce its own indigenous supermen. First, it had to recruit and attract volunteers, mainly among bored veteran officers and NCOs form other IDF *Sayarot*, "reconnaissance formations," as well as new conscripts: idealistic eighteen year olds, who would be willing and able to undergo over a year of hell and sign on an additional few years of military service as professional soldiers in demanding unit. Unit 669 also needed a special breed of medical personnel to volunteer—flight surgeons and doctors in search of a challenging change to their careers. According to Lieutenant-Colonel B., a thirty-nine-year-old flight surgeon and helicopter pilot, as well as one-time Unit 669 commander, the response to "the call for volunteers, initially, was so great that our ranks were filled quite quickly—I was even forced to tell friends who graduated with me in medical school and ahead of me in officer's course that we didn't need any more personnel."

Training in Unit 669 lasts over a year and is probably the most arduous, demanding, and all inclusive in the IDF. Unit 669 team members have to be a little bit of everything. They have to be expert medics to support the team's flight surgeon; first aid and cardiopulmonary resuscitation (CPR) are much-honed staples of Unit 669 training. As many of their rescue attempts must be made in enemy territory, amid a flurry of projectile and warhead activity, Unit 669 team members have to

A tandem of Unit 669 Bell-212s race low above a snow-covered hilltop in southern Lebanon. (Biton Heyl Ha'Avir)

be expert soldiers, able to make it toward a wounded pilot's or soldier's position as well as to hightail it out of there in haste; they are trained to be intimate, comfortable, and deadly with every type of weapon—Israeli, Soviet, American, European, and "other"-found within the IAF's range, a geographical limit that, although classified, includes many countries throughout the Middle East and parts of Europe, Asia, and Africa.

All Unit 669 soldiers must know how to kill as well as heal. Because the Israeli military operations are carried out almost daily and pass well beyond the boundaries of the State of Israel, Unit 669 must perform under all climatic and geographic conditions. Its personnel are full-fledged static-line and HALO paratroopers; expert rappellers and mountaineers; well-trained drivers, skiers, cold-weather survivalists, scuba divers, and sailors; and superb combat swimmers. They are also expert at demolitions; when a pilot—and plane—are downed, Unit 669 commandos must know just how much explosive it will take to obliterate a top-secret aircraft before the enemy can come and retrieve it. They also have to know the intricacies of antipersonnel and antitank land mines, since pilots in the past have landed in mine fields. Most important, perhaps, Unit 669's pilots and ground crews must be the best the IAF can field—able to fly and maintain helicopters for long-range operations, in conditions ranging from the brutal heat of the Negev Desert to the snowy cold of the Lebanon mountain range.

Unit 669's primary mode of transportation was, for nearly twenty years, the Bell-212 and the CH-53 *Yasur*—although it can deploy from fixed-wing aircraft, such as the Arava and the C-130 Hercules. Its aircraft are airborne operating rooms and mini arsenals, equipped with a wide variety of both medical and offensive military hardware, which enables them to be ready to handle any eventuality at a moment's notice. The type of aircraft deployed depends on the type of incident Unit 669 is called to, as well as on the condition of the patient. The flight surgeons, for example, prefer the *Yasur* for delicate injuries because it is big and comfortable, quiet with a steady flight, and relatively free from oil leaks. The Bell-212 are more maneuverable, but they tend to vibrate too much in flight-making the performance of some delicate medical procedures a precarious undertaking. Recently, however, the UH-60A Blackhawk has become the unit's chief mode of transportation. All Unit 669 choppers are equipped with the Air Mobile Life Support Unit (AMLSU), a system specifically designed by the IDF's *Heyl Refuah*, "Medical Corps." The AMLSU transforms a helicopter into a flying coronary intensive care unit. It contains oxygen storage of approximately 520 gallons and respiratory resuscitation equipment; a cardiac monitor and defibrillator; suction and aspiration equipment; and auxiliary equipment for illumination, storage and control. Besides being advanced, it is a practical device. It can perform cardiac monitoring and defibrillation on one patient, positive pressure ventilation of two patients, and oxygen enrichment to two others—simultaneously! The AMLSU has already saved dozens of lives, including those of three seriously wounded soldiers trapped behind Hizbollah lines in Lebanon.

A F-15 driver climbs into his aircraft—ready to execute his mission to the latter and realizing that Unit 669 is on hand to pick him up out of any situation should he be shot down or be forced to ditch his aircraft. (Biton Heyl Ha'Avir)

Unit 669's versatile equipment allows the unit to be mobile and fast: endearing qualities when the difference between life and death can be measured in seconds. In peacetime, Unit 669 is spread out among several air bases in Israel. When the siren is sounded and the crews race toward the awaiting choppers, they have no idea whether they are going to be rescuing an injured Phantom pilot who has been shot down by SAMs over Lebanon or the victims of a terrorist incident in a northern frontier

A Unit 669 CH-53 lifts off at a sharp, and almost impossible climb, during live-fire training exercises in the Negev Desert. (Biton Heyl Ha'Avir)

Unit 669 operators train in the middle of the Mediterranean with an IDF/Navy Dabur patrol boat. (Biton Heyl Ha'Avir)

town. They get a priority takeoff form the control tower every time. Only after they are airborne does the pilot get the first tidbits of information regarding where he'll be flying to and what his crew will be doing. Each and every job is attended to with dire seriousness—full combat loads are taken on each sortie, from CAR-15 5.56mm assault rifles, to LAW rockets.

Until 1982, most of Unit 669's combat expertise went untested. The unit's Bell-212s had hovered amid blinding clouds of smoke, and rescuers dangled by rope into a fiery hell while freeing tourists from an inferno in the luxurious Hotel Moriah on the shores of the Dead Sea. They had saved dehydrated and critically injured hikers who fell down deep crevices in the Negev Desert; and, until Israel's pullout from the Sinai Desert, they had delivered countless bouncing baby girls and boys from Bedouins who trusted no doctor other than "the masked medicine men who arrived by flying monster." All that changed on June 6, 1982. For Unit 669, as for much of the IAF in the eighties, the moment of truth came in Lebanon, during Operation Peace for Galilee.

On the first day of the war, a day that was particularly brutal for the IAF, Unit 669 executed a spectacular rescue. During the late morning blitz, an IAF Skyhawk was downed by a SAM-7; the pilot's body was seized by the Palestinian terrorists who shot him down, savagely mutilated, and then, to the delight of television news crews, paraded through the streets of the city of Sidon-dangling out of a car trunk. In the afternoon, a Bell-212 Unit 669 chopper flying over the Nabatiyeh Plateau, in southern Lebanon, was hit by Palestinian ground fire and shot down as it raced to rescue a downed Skyhawk pilot eventually captured by PLO units. All five crew members were killed, however, and the body of the chopper pilot was dragged through the streets of Tyre and mutilated. Later that night, Unit 669 unit commanded by Lieutenant-Colonel R., from the same Bell-212 squadron of the chopper downed

Operators ferry a wounded comrade down a gorge near the Lebanese frontier. (Bamachane)

During training, one of the unit's premier "toughening-up" tools is a series of endless forced marches. Here, unit hopefuls endure a forty-kilometer trek in the heart of a Middle East summer. (Bamachane)

Operators deploy from the cargo hold of an IAF CH-53 in southern Lebanon. (Bamachane)

earlier, was assigned a mission: gravely wounded soldiers from the Sayeret Golani task force-the reconnaissance commando battalion of the 1st Golani Infantry Brigade-who had participated in the capture of Beaufort Castle a few hours earlier were awaiting the medevac trip back to a hospital in northern Israel. The battle for Beaufort Castle was still going, however; mopping-up operations were still underway and the area was still very hot. To make matters worse, the precise location of the wounded Golani commandos was not known. To add to an already tense situation that was developing in Lieutenant-Colonel R.'s Bell-212, they'd be flying into the same aerial zone in which the Bell-212 flown by their friends had been blown out of the sky.

Even though such a rescue was something rehearsed in training thousands of times, nothing is like the real thing: what Israelis call *Tachlis*! The skies were cloudy and visibility was minimal. The Bell-212 landed and pulled up at several rendezvous points, only to find no friendly forces anywhere in the immediate vicinity. Radio communications with the Golani force failed to establish its exact coordinates, and the rescue pilots were forced to locate it by a slow, nerve-racking, low-altitude search below the safety of cloud cover. After thirty minutes of searching, under intense Palestinian ground fire, the Bell-212 finally spotted the Golani fighters. Unit 669 crew hastily loaded the wounded on board, attended to their medical conditions, and shot like the devil out of Lebanon.

During the flight back to Israel, and a hospital in Safed, the Bell-212 found itself the target of incessant gun and missile fire. Major F., one of the Bell-212's pilots, found himself maneuvering in and out of tracer lines, under and above mortar shells, and amid a whole host of lights and explosions even his trained eye couldn't identify. To shore up his—as well as the rest of the crew's—courage, he was heard joking over the radio, "I don't think they like us up here." For the following 12 hours, Lieutenant-Colonel R.'s Bell-212—and a few other aircraft form the squadron-shuttled back and forth to southern Lebanon to evacuated dozens of other seriously wounded soldiers.

Later that year, Lieutenant-Colonel R.'s crew was cited by Major-General David Ivry, the IAF commanding officer during Operation Peace for Galilee, "for dedication to mission in the face of hazardous ground fire and equally hazardous atmospheric conditions, and for demonstration of high standard of professional skill." Lieutenant-Colonel R. viewed this appreciation as a loud and clear message to the soldiers on the ground that should they ever find themselves in a situation where they need help from above, Unit 669 will spare no effort to evacuate them to a hospital as quickly as humanly possible. In Lieutenant-Colonel R.'s words, "If we succeed in alleviating some of the anxiety of our forces on the ground, we have more than performed our mission."

Other Unit 669 teams proved just as impressive in Lebanon. During the first four months of Operation Peace for Galilee, eighty-five percent of Israeli casualties were evacuated by air for the forty-five minute flight

In a recreation of one of the air force's most famous rescues, in October 1986, a pilot is plucked to safety courtesty of an IAF Bell-209 Cobra. (Biton Heyl Ha'Avir)

back to Israel; a total of 2,518 medevac trips were made by chopper—a marked accomplishment compared with the 1973 war when only thirty percent of the Israeli wounded were medevaced. Sometimes, the severity of a soldier's wounded did not afford Unit 669 pilots the "luxury" of the hour ride back to Israel, and they had to fly to a safe location somewhat removed from the fighting; the flight surgeons performed emergency surgery in the field while shells landed nearby, and Unit 669 personnel took up firing positions to protect the impromptu operating room from enemy attack. One of Unit 669's greatest regrets of its operations in Lebanon was not being able to retrieve Captain Ron Arad, a Phantom navigator, shot down over Lebanon in 1986. The Phantom's pilot was plucked up in a dramatic rescue on the landing skids of an AH-1S Cobra. Ron Arad was captured by Shiite gunmen, turned over to Hizbollah, and today he is believed held in Teheran by Iranian intelligence.

For many Unit 669 doctors, reservists brought into the fray for a month or two annually, the transition is sharp and dramatic. Only days earlier, they were wearing white lab coats, treating common colds, and tending to fussy patients in clinics in Tel Aviv, Jerusalem, or Haifa. Now, in the unit, with their flight coveralls, full battle kit, personal weapon, and commando knife, they are performing lifesaving emergency surgical procedures on a slab of dirt in Lebanon, trying to stabilize a body ripped by shrapnel so that a wounded soldier can survive the flight back to Israel.

The difficult psychological transition for the citizen-soldier-reservist relies on a built-in human strength that Unit 669's intense pre-acceptance screening process hopes to, but can't always, determine in a candidate. According to Major D., a senior flight surgeon and seasoned veteran of countless Lebanon sorties, "we try desperately hard to draw the fine golden line between the quickness of the evac and what's medically safe. The golden line also separates the civilian doctors from the reservist or career Unit 669 flight surgeon."

Unit 669 rescues were not limited solely to IDF personnel; severely wounded Lebanese citizens, Syrian soldiers, and Palestinian terrorists

A CH-53 crewman readies a line to a trapped group of special operations unit commandos during an exercise in central Israel. (IDF)

were also lifted by helicopter out of Lebanon to Israeli hospitals. The end of Operation Peace for Galilee did not end the IDF's involvement in Lebanon, however, and Unit 669 operations continued-as always, around the clock. Unit 669's all-encompassing training paid invaluable dividends in the difficult climatic conditions encountered in Israel's neighbor up north-bitter cold and blizzard snows in the winter and brutal heat in the summer-with Unit 669 teams forced to use all their specialized gear.

Perhaps Unit 669's most pressing day in Lebanon was on May 4, 1988, when a large IDF paratrooper force attacked the Hizbollah stronghold in the village of Maidun in southeastern Lebanon, in retaliation for Hizbollah's assistance to numerous Palestinian attempts to infiltrate suicide terrorist squads into northern Israel. The battle was so fierce that many fire-fights were conducted at pointblank ranges, the Hizbollah gunmen not surrendering their positions until they were martyred by superior IDF fire-power. Three Israeli paratroopers were killed in the chaos and seventeen were seriously wounded. Each Israeli casualty was medevaced to safety by Unit 669, its Bell-212s landing on numerous occasions into murderous hails of Shiite machine gun and cannon fire. Exchange of fire was so incessant that many of the door gunners ran out of 7.62 millimeter ammunition for their FN MAGs. Many senior IAF commanders consider Unit 669's performance at Maidun to be the unit's most difficult test, and one of its most shining successes.

On the quiet days, where no news from Lebanon is good news-what's basically known in Israel as peacetime-Unit 669 is always on alert and always ready. Peacetime does not bring a much-needed vacation to the unit, however. Training exercises, civilian accidents, and other dangerous situations always requires attention. When a hiker realizes he cannot get down from a mountain he has scaled in the Arava Desert, Unit 669 plucks him to safety. When a severe traffic accident occurs on Israel's chaotic roads, Unit 669 is the first one called; its ability to pry a victim loose from mangled steel impresses even the most experienced civilian

A Unit 669 operator prepares for a water rescue exercise. (Biton Heyl Ha'Avir)

firefighters and paramedics. And when an organ is needed for a transplant, Unit 669 pilots are offered the chance to become high-flying, high-speed, aerial taxi drivers.

Military training accidents and mishaps also need to be contended with. Recently on maneuvers, a commando from a reconnaissance unit fell into a sand pit that was over twenty-five-feet deep. Soldiers form the unit tried in vain to extract their comrade from the hole, but he was seriously hurt form the fall and not responding to their attempts. Finally, Unit 669 was summoned. To the awe of the commandos on the ground, a flight surgeon was lowered into the deep pit and came out moments later with the wounded soldier safely in specially designed folding stretcher. At last report, both soldier and unit were doing fine.

During the bloody apex of the Intifadah, the first Palestinian uprising in the West Bank and Gaza Strip, Unit 669 was operational and active almost twenty-four-hours-per-day, evacuating Israeli soldiers trapped in hostile environs who were wounded and in desperate need of medical attention.

The ability of Unit 669 to execute such difficult and delicate missions comes as a result of the high quality of volunteers. Historically, Unit 669 sought its personnel from new conscripts at the IDF's main recruitment depot, but according to the unit's commander in the early nineties, Major N., "We've gone away from the traditional method of seeking potential volunteers of being a combat rescuer in out unit, by searching computer files, by now seeking those soldiers who find themselves suddenly expelled from pilot's course and still very much wanting to remain in the Air Force. Not to say that all ex-pilot cadets are suitable for Unit 669 service, but we generally find in them a motivational high and a desire to prove themselves that few other Israeli soldiers can emulate."

The doctors, on the other hand, are interesting enigmas. They have to be studious geniuses, able to master basic medicine and emergency trauma care, as well as Rambo-like commandos, able to fire dozens of different weapons, march endless kilometers, scale steep cliffs, and then find the wherewithal to administer expert medical care to a critically hurt individual. The doctors, elitist and temperamental persons in any culture, love the thrill and danger. This is especially true with the reservists who check out hernias one afternoon and save a downed and frostbitten pilot the next. Soon, in a landmark decision by IAF OC Major-General Eitan Ben-Eliyahu, women medics are soon to fly into the hell of Lebanon on assignments with their male counterparts.

According to published accounts, the IAF possesses three distinctive "special operations" elements—including two top-secret units that land behind enemy lines in order to pin-point targets for oncoming fighter-bombers. Yet Unit 669 is different—it is a force that virtually every segment of Israeli society appreciates and values. Even though an air of

A F-16 trainer takes off during a mock-support exercise designed to teach close-combat maneuvers to pilots when operating in tandem with a Unit 669 rescue. (Biton Heyl Ha'Avir)

military secrecy hovers over the unit and much of Unit 669's operations are top-secret, it is the one IAF unit with regular contact with the civilian population. It is also the one IAF unit that ground units welcome with open arms. Yet of all the special operations units within the IAF command, the F-15 and F-16 pilots enjoy a special bond with the commandos of "669." "These are the guys who will come and rescue me if I get shot down," claims Captain L., an F-15 pilot operating out of a base in central Israel, "if I end up in enemy territory, alone, and armed with little more than a pistol and my wits, it's going to be these twenty-year-olds, these reservist doctors, and these chopper pilots who'll be the difference between me coming home to see my wife and baby girl, or ending up in captivity, in the hands of a Hizbollah torturer. The remarkable thing to me about these specialist soldiers is the fact that they don't view you as a higher-ranking officer, or as someone who, on the base might even have yelled at them. To them, you are a patient and a challenge. And, they don't let patients die and they rarely fail in a challenge!"

Spring 1998, less than twenty-four hours before the onset of *Yom Ha'Zikaron,* the solemn day in which the State of Israel honors its 18,748 war dead, Unit 669 was once again airborne, and in the line of fire, to ensure that the death toll to Israel's long roll call of war fallen did not grow. In the heaviest fighting in southern Lebanon of 1998, a force of reconnaissance infantrymen from the *Na'ha'l* Brigade waged a night-long battle with a special operations unit of Hizbollah guerrillas in the Karkum zone in the western stretches of the "security zone" after they had been ambushed. The brigade doctor suffered a critical shrapnel wounded to the head, and two other soldiers were critically hurt. A 669 chopper was summoned immediately. It was a classic Hizbollah ambush, and it appeared as if the target they were after was the 669 chopper—the only clearing in the field of fire was booby-trapped with explosive devices. As a result, amid the fog of southern Lebanon, the smoke of a fire-fight, and the ricocheting hell of thousands of rounds of enemy ordnance whizzing past their ears and their chopper, the rescue helicopter couldn't land. As it hovered precariously amid the explosions and machine gun fire, a 669 rescue team lowered a stretcher by winch from the helicopter's cabin and raised the three most badly hurt soldiers one by one. According to Captain A., the chopper's pilot, "I steadied the chopper ever so carefully, and the rescue commandos raced down to the ground to load the wounded onto the stretchers. We constantly train for just such scenarios, and I was relieved that under fire, we carried out our mission exactly like we do on maneuvers."

It is early morning at the unit's classified home-base in central Israel, and the sun's first reassuring rays are met by the roars and sonic booms of jet fighters_taking off and landing at the bustling airfield. Posters celebrating Israel's fiftieth anniversary still decorate the living quarters and recreation room, though most of the unit's operators realize that the next fifty years have already begun and although a peace process exists, the motto of the team is pray for peace and prepare for war. It is impossible to gauge when and where the unit's next assignment will happen, and if the IAF's range and Israel's strategic concerns are any hint, the unit could find itself on call to deploy literally anywhere in the region. Yet at their home base, senior commanders attend to the unit's rigorous training schedule, flight mechanics ready the choppers for war, and the pilots stand at the ready, on-call for a flight into harm's way. The operators start their day readying their weaponry and equipment, catching up on the latest emergency medical news, and listening, ever so intently to news reports on the radio and for the siren that will propel them into action.

A female flight officer readies a rescue team's gear on board a unit chopper. (IAF)

Footnote:
Unit 669 has, in its illustrious history, always been at the ready to rescue soldiers and fellow citizens, at any place and at any time. They have helped rescue soldiers under fire in southern Lebanon and they have helped to deliver babies in Bedouin encampments in the Negev Desert. But after peace with the Palestinians was thought of as a "done deal," unit operators never thought that they would be summoned to help an embattled group of settlers caught in a Palestinian ambush, and they never thought that the 7.62mm fire their choppers would absorb would come from the guns of the Palestinian intelligence services.

But, on October 19, 2000, during the Palestinian's "al-Aqsa Intifadah," Israeli troops seeking to rescue wounded settlers waged a deadly battle with Palestinian gunmen for five hours Friday on a rocky West Bank hill. The battle on Mount Ebal overlooking Nablus killed one Palestinian and wounded at least five others. Six Jewish settlers were hit by gunfire, as unit rescue helicopters succeeded in evacuating only two. Settlers said the wounded were in moderate to serious condition. The rescue helicopters came under murderous Palestinian gunfire, and unit operators were forced to return fire. Two IAF attack helicopters hovered over the scene, though they limited their fire to 20mm cannon rounds.

All the unit assets returned to their bases in good order, though the incident (described as a cease-fire violation) was nothing short of a full-scale battle the likes of which Unit 669 had not seen since the height of the operations against Hizbollah in Lebanon.